Make It Happen

Mitch Clark
1998 NCAA Champion at 177 lbs.

Make It Happen

The Inspiring Story of an NCAA Wrestling Champion

By
Mitch Clark
and Scott Conroe

Published by
White Pillars Press
P.O. Box 185
Canton, N.Y. 13617

Manufactured in the United States of America

Cover photograph by John Clark
Cover design by Richard Austin
Interior design by Juliann Smiley
Interior photographs by John Clark, Scott Conroe, Steve Parker
    and H. Peter Venier
Edited and typeset by John N. Serio

ISBN 0-9675492-0-5

Printed on recycled paper

*This book is dedicated to
my family for their support from
pee-wee to present and
to those who have been an inspiration
from day one. — You know who you are.*

And to all of those who wrestle.

Table of Contents

Foreword

My personal perception of life has been molded greatly by my involvement in the sport of wrestling for over 35 years. I wrestled through high school and college and was fortunate to have represented the United States in Pan American, World and Olympic competition from 1971 to 1980.

The most meaningful and emotional moments of my athletic life, however, have occurred as a coach. Nothing I ever attained as a competitor could come even close to the magnitude of the enjoyment and satisfaction that have come from sitting matside when one of my college wrestlers earns an NCAA wrestling title.

There is something most rewarding in watching a champion claim long sought, personal glory and knowing you had some influence, however small, in helping him get there.

It never gets old. Ever!

Mitch Clark earned his title most recently in 1998, and his experiences throughout his wrestling career shared in this book will inspire and motivate you.

I was proud to be his coach.

I knew Mitch's parents before he was even born. Mitch's father, John, was himself a great coach at St. Lawrence University. I worked his wrestling camps in Canton, New York, throughout the mid-1970s into the 1980s. I was always impressed with the way John touched the lives of so many through devoted, organized and unselfish efforts year in and year out for the betterment of wrestlers and wrestling.

I am not surprised that his son was a National Champion.

Exceptional achievers, like Mitch, are fanatics. They exude confidence. Their winning qualities are inherent, obvious, irrepressible and totally unstoppable. They crave competition and perform at their best when confronted with it. They respect other's success and learn from it. They demand discipline. Commitment for them is total and complete. They never compromise.

They make you believe. Again!

They may have a different face, a different personality, a different demeanor, a different style, but the outcome is always the same. They win!

Mitch wanted to be a national champion the first day he wrestled at Ohio State. I never doubted him.

Wrestlers cannot be successful without a willingness to work very hard and sacrifice the average life-styles and interests of the general population. This becomes more difficult to do all the time in our society. Fewer and fewer people are willing to *mentally*, *emotionally*, and *physically* give everything they possess to attain specific goals. Most don't even set the goals.

Mitch never faltered in his quest and always knew the greatest joy, the greatest satisfaction, the greatest contentment and the greatest personal pride come from exhaustive, taxing work that results in great achievement.

Champions, like Mitch, recognize the value of a certain mentality and voluntarily abandon the negatives and pursue the challenges of a meaningful, attainable but elevated goal. I truly believe that the key to becoming great is to train excessively and enthusiastically because you *want* to, not because you have to.

Mitch was always prepared to put wrestling first.

No one ever wanted to win more than Mitch. I do not believe Mitch was very often the most talented guy on the mat, but I know he always expected to win anyway. There is much to be learned from that type of attitude.

This book tells a great story, Mitch's story. We can all benefit from his observations and insights. I hope you get as much enjoyment and satisfaction from reading Mitch's story as I did in coaching him.

Russ Hellickson, Head Coach
Ohio State University

Part I

My Story

Every Wrestling Career
Is a Journey

(Mitch)

The day I reached the biggest goal of my life, to become a national collegiate champion in wrestling, I felt it coming. I just knew.

The NCAA Division I championship bouts were on March 20, 1998, at Cleveland State University. The whole three-day tournament was everything you'd expect: roaring crowds that filled an enormous arena, drama everywhere, referees' whistles and coaches' yells, television cameras and news photographers. It was like a state tournament times four in its intensity. And there I was at the center of it: fifth-year senior at Ohio State, seeded first at 177 pounds, with a 38–1 record for the season, two-time Big Ten champion, 1997 NCAA runner-up. Usually I might feel everyone watching me. I'd been ranked No. 1 all season, lost only once (in my final home dual meet, of all times). But I'd learned my lesson about major tournaments: take it one match at a time, try to ignore the rest of it, put aside the glory so it wouldn't overwhelm me as it had the year before. Now I had only one more bout, against Vertus Jones, a sophomore from West Virginia who was seeded sixth.

I felt confident as I rode to the arena with my coaches. The early challenges were behind me: those first two bouts, which are always dangerous to any wrestler who is seeded high; the 6–4 nail-biter in the quarterfinal against Penn State's Rob Neidlinger, who'd always given me problems; the 5–0 semifinal win over Pittsburgh's John Withrow. I'd spent the day shopping at a mall with my family, bought some clothing, tried to think about other things besides wrestling. You can exhaust yourself at a major tournament if you spend too much time watching bouts or walking around. You have to get away. I'd been in the finals before, so I knew what to expect.

I probably cracked a few jokes. I always grew more relaxed as I advanced through a tournament. That year I'd become one of those guys who always tried to keep everyone loose. Every team needs someone like that, especially late in the season.

In the last five blocks, as we flipped the radio dial, we came upon one of our team's theme songs: "Make It Happen" by Mariah Carey. I heard the main verse: "If you get down on your knees at night and pray to the Lord, He's going to make it happen." It then goes on to say, "If you believe and know that you can, you're going to make it happen." Christianity has been important in my life, a well of strength to turn to at times. When I heard that song, it was clear to me that I'd win.

The rest of it passed so quickly. In the parking lot I saw Jason Robison of Edinboro University, a finalist at 190, who had been my friend since we toured Europe with a junior national team in high school. Jason looked so nervous. Usually he was the calm one. As I entered the arena I saw the crowd and the elevated mat, and sensed the atmosphere, and suddenly my relaxed mood began to waver. But I loved being part of it all: the NCAA championships. My family was there, in the Ohio State contingent, with about 20 friends, relatives and people from back home in northern New York. My best friend from home had flown in from Scotland. Having so many people there for me added a little pressure, but mostly it was just a nice thing, one more reason to win.

My mother came over to me as I warmed up, which was a surprise. She always left me alone before matches, partly because she felt out of her element and partly because wrestling was my father's domain. She always gave me verses from Scripture before I wrestled, and I tucked them in my sock. Usually she passed the verse to me through a trainer or teammate. But this time she gave it to me herself. She'd been up early that morning, reading the Bible, and she felt strongly that I'd win. Her verse was from Psalm 20: "May He give you the desire of your heart and make all your plans succeed. We will shout for joy when you are victorious and lift up our banner in the name of God."

I got in The Zone, which is what I call my state of totally concentrating on what needs to be done.

I got in The Zone, and I beat Vertus Jones by technical fall in the first period, 18–0, a first in NCAA Championships history.

I'd like to tell you about the match itself, but I have little memory of it.

On videotape I see Jones get behind me while we're standing, a point in the match where he could try a takedown. He doesn't. Then I take him down to his back for five points and crank away from on top, tilting him to his back until the referee signals the end, because of my 18–0 advantage, about one second before the first period ends. I see myself point to the sky as I stand up, pointing to God. I point to the Ohio State part of the crowd. I walk over to my coaches, and our head coach Russ Hellickson says, "That was awesome." I see myself holding back waves of emotion during my interview with ESPN. I don't hug or pat Russ or Ken Ramsey, our chief assistant coach, and that bothers me. I mean, Russ has been like my second father. But I guess I was in The Zone so deeply, I was geared up to go three periods and couldn't break out of it.

I was just relieved to have it done with, after all those years of working hard, of trying to overcome the barriers between me and achievement in wrestling, of aiming at high goals and coming up short. I was tired of being the bridesmaid.

I wanted throughout high school to be the first wrestler from my section of New York State to be a state champion. I failed, taking second twice. My younger brother Johnny reached that goal instead, two weeks before my win in the NCAA finals.

I wasn't a state champ in high school, but I was a national champ. Go figure. It just shows that some of the best things in life are unexpected.

The national tournament is for high school seniors. I went to that tournament two weeks after losing the state final in overtime, after having my biggest dream ripped from my grasp and crumpled. I wasn't sure I'd place in the national tournament, because I'd injured my sternum and everyone in every weight class was a stud, accustomed to success.

But I decided to go. And I won. I pinned four of my opponents, including the Maryland state champ whom I faced in the finals. He was leading, and I chose top, and I pinned him.

I almost always chose top after that.

Six of the guys in my weight class went on to become college All-Americans. My high school put a huge portrait of me in the gym. Know what, though? Even becoming a high school national champion didn't quite soothe the pain of losing in the state final two weeks earlier.

I started at Ohio State as a true freshman and was 15–5 . . . and then was declared academically ineligible. I dreamed of a national championship in college . . . and missed as a junior. I reached my senior year at

OSU as the favorite to be the national champion in my weight class . . . and injured a knee, which could have ended the whole thing.

I'm not whining. I'm just saying that, before I stood in the center of that arena in Cleveland and had my arm raised in victory, a lot of things went wrong. My father says a wrestling career is a journey, filled with moments of joy and agony. Life itself is like that.

This is the story of one wrestler's journey, through good times and painful times, to the pinnacle of college sport. It's about being an athlete in college and, in particular, the Big Ten, the toughest conference in wrestling and one of the tougher conferences in any sport. It's about finding ways to make up for whatever you lack, about striving toward goals and, if you don't reach them, licking your wounds, knowing you tried and choosing new goals.

My high school coach says every wrestler is the product of several coaches. To that I would add teammates, family and mentors such as teachers or people from the community. These people, from my hometown of Canton, New York, and from Ohio State, are part of this too. They are part of who I am.

This story is filled with my thoughts about a lot of things, but I can't pretend to have insights into everything.

I've never wrestled a girl, so I don't know what to tell anyone about wrestling the opposite sex.

I don't know about dealing with abusive parents or broken homes or poverty or living on the edge. Many wrestlers contend with tough family situations, with a lack of love, with friends who lead them to crime or drugs. It wasn't like that for me. My parents, John and Donna, raised seven children with the means to send them to college and give them a comfortable life (I'm the third child and oldest boy). We lived several miles from the nearest village, in a farmhouse, and for several years we had some livestock, so there were always household chores. But that wasn't too rough. My parents weren't big TV fans, still aren't, so we spent a lot of time together, entertaining ourselves. We never doubted we were loved. I was a handful as a boy, and sometimes my father hit me, but I never was in trouble with the law. So, on the subjects of parents and poverty, my thoughts are limited.

There are plenty of things I'll talk about, though.

I'll talk about looking at the people around you to see who you are. It's easy in the practice room. One thing about wrestling, it shows you who you are, and it shows everybody else too. There's a team, but it's not out there on the mat with you. Away from wrestling, you see yourself reflected in others, and you have their perspectives to absorb.

I'll talk about losing weight, which is an enormous part of wrestling's discipline. At times, I had to drop so many pounds that I was weak, dizzy, thirsty enough to drink a lake. It used to upset my mother and my teachers. I'm not sorry I did it. The sport has changed now, with new rules about weight classes, and new weight classes in college. I'd be at 184 or 197 now. But you still have to be able to control your weight.

I'll talk about absorbing defeat. Every wrestler has to learn that early, but some defeats are harder to get past in your mind than others.

I'll talk about dealing with the news media. We didn't have much of it in the rural region where I grew up, but we had enough. I attracted a lot of attention, as John Clark's son, as a potential state champion. I learned to talk to writers and TV people. I faced even more of this at Ohio State, where football and basketball get most of the press but other sports attract their share.

I'll talk about distractions. People think college athletes have unbelievable social lives, but it isn't so. You have to spend so much time at practice, at weight-lifting sessions, losing weight, traveling. You have schoolwork. I remember a Friday night in my senior year when I stopped at a convenience store to buy something, and four Ohio State students were on their way to a social event. They were out to have a good time, and I was on my way to the gym to ride the bike, to lose some pounds. At the same time, you have friends, and girls, and fans, all vying for your attention. You have people who don't like wrestling, asking why you'd spend your life on this sport that they think is stupid. Through all of it, you have to focus.

I'll talk about the pressures that come with being ranked, whether it's regionally or statewide or nationally. Rankings for teams and individual wrestlers help to build interest in our sport, but they can wear on you.

I'll talk about looking inside yourself when you fail and when you succeed.

I'll talk about discovering what you have and what you don't, as an athlete. I may be a national champion in a demanding sport, but I'm not gifted by any means. My two younger brothers have more natural coordination, quickness, sheer ability. Johnny succeeded where I failed, becoming the first guy from our section to win a state title, as a junior, two weeks before I won the NCAA title. He won at 145, and I'm much bigger, a finalist at 155 and 167, so it's hard to compare. I was a little envious, but also very happy that someone from our family did it.

I'll talk about getting past obstacles. A lot of the best wrestlers come from high schools or regions that breed champions in our sport. My high school, Canton Central, has turned out state champions in hockey, boys' soccer, and state contenders in soccer and boys' lacrosse, but wrestling is a small sport there. People in Ohio hear I'm from New York and they think of New York City, but New York City is seven hours from Canton, which is in St. Lawrence County. You have to go through the Adirondacks. Canton is actually northwest of Lake Placid. The nearest big cities are Canadian: Montreal and Ottawa. Only seven schools in my section have wrestling, so it's hard to find the sort of competition that pushes you to the level where you can be a state champion. My father found a way to push me, and later Johnny, and I'll talk about that too.

I'm not built like many wrestlers. I'm 6-foot-3, long and lean, and over the years I learned to use my body as a lever. As you might guess, I was more vulnerable on my feet, so I both worked to improve on my feet and mastered the techniques of being on top. I'm what coaches call funky, unorthodox. I learned to see openings, feel shifts in balance beyond the fundamentals we're all taught. My teammates say I do things that make them look at each other and say, "What did I just see?" I have a hard time explaining it, but I'll try. Some of what I do comes from my imagination. I'm five years older than the next male child in my family, Johnny, and we lived out in the country, so I often played alone as a boy. It helped me become more imaginative and, as I looked for ways to win, to see things other wrestlers didn't.

So, this is one wrestler's story. I'll tell you what happened to me, and what I think about some of the problems or situations that young athletes face. I'll talk about training methods, high points and low points, my parents and friends and coaches and teammates. It was a journey, all right, and some parts of it will resemble every wrestler's journey. It begins where we all do, with learning what wrestling is and with being kids.

Ω

Where Goals and Work
Ethic Mattered

(Scott)

Wrestlers are both born to their sport and shaped by what their coaches teach them. By that I mean a wrestler spends years learning fundamentals, and then the weapons in his arsenal and the mental approach that helps him endure the bad times, but he's also born to be a wrestler. As a boy he likes to get physical, roll around with his brothers or friends on the living room floor, tackle people.

Mitch Clark was born to wrestle, and then he was shaped by his teachers, before he was an NCAA champion for Ohio State.

I'm Scott Conroe, the other narrator of Mitch's story. I'll be the voice of some chapters, when Mitch is too modest to talk about himself or when other people talk about him.

Among other things, I've been a sports writer for the Syracuse newspapers in Syracuse, New York, about three hours south of where Mitch and I grew up. I wrote about high school and college athletes. I wrote a lot about wrestling, because I love it. The editors used to send me to cover the high school sectional and state tournaments almost every year, because nobody else on the staff liked the sport as much as I did. I've been hooked on wrestling, and on photographing it, since the 1973–74 season. I was a freshman at St. Lawrence University in Canton, New York, the small college where Mitch's dad coached wrestling, was later athletic director and is now a liaison for the building of new sports facilities and a development officer specializing in raising money from alumni who were athletes. I was from Potsdam, 10 miles away. All I knew about wrestling was that my high school had a strong team, though I'd never been to a match, and that I was always glad when I got past our two days of wrestling in junior high physical education class. When our teacher made us wrestle, he showed us basic moves, but we still didn't have a clue what we were doing. We'd have a tournament, lightest boy going first, one at a time until one boy won it all. The champion was always the biggest and strongest. In ninth grade, it was someone from the junior varsity wrestling team; we had four JV wrestlers in our class. The only time I won a match in that physical education class, in ninth grade, I won by pin, and for a few seconds I felt the incredible elation that wrestlers feel. Then the kid said he had let me pin him. He just wanted to coast through class with a minimum of effort. So that was the end of my wrestling career. But, without remembering exactly why, for the next 29 years I understood that joy on the faces of wrestlers as they won.

Canton and Potsdam each have two colleges. None of the four has wrestling now, so there are no college wrestlers in that region for youngsters to watch and emulate. St. Lawrence was the last of the four to drop the sport, after the 1994–95 season. John Clark, Mitch's dad, was the athletic director by then, after more than 20 years as coach, and it just crushed him to see it go. He'd built that program into one of the best in NCAA Division III, guiding the Saints to a national title in 1988 and nine individual wrestlers to national titles. This was sad for many of us St. Lawrence alumni, and I only bring it up because it's a good place to start: a man driven to build things and to work as hard as he needed to, in order to succeed, and a practice room where a young boy grew up around wrestlers, knowing the sport since he can remember.

Mitch was born in June 1975, when I was entering my junior year at SLU. Two sisters came before him, Christy and Nicki, and after him came Sarah, Johnny, Mary and Charlie. Their parents, John and Donna, were achievers — each was chosen Most Likely to Succeed in high school — and raised their children to be achievers. John was the first sectional champion for his high school in Fulton, New York, which is about two hours south of Canton, near Lake Ontario's south shore. He was an early part of what grew into one of New York's premier wrestling programs that were later coached by men that John had coached at SLU. He wrestled for SLU and was a conference champion as a senior in 1969. He got his master's degree at SLU and met his wife, Donna Reid of Ramsey, New Jersey, who was his classmate, and a few years after graduating, he took over as head coach of wrestling. The Clarks eventually bought a farmhouse between Canton and the tiny village of Dekalb Junction. There's a long driveway, and a barn where John kept chickens and horses, and fields where John set down 60 beehives. That big house, surrounded by fields, on a back road in the country, is where Mitch grew up.

Canton is a village of about 7,000, the county seat of St. Lawrence County, a huge patchwork of farmland, forest and tundra. Our county is so remote and rural, it has about 1.5 people per square mile. There's one city, Ogdensburg, which has only about 15,000 people. The nearest big-

Country home where the Clark family raised seven children

ger cities, other than the ones across the border in Canada, are Watertown (over an hour south), Syracuse (two hours south) and Burlington, Vt. (three hours north and east).

The Clarks made a family foundation of sports, school, Christianity, work ethic and a quest for achievement tempered by humility. Like all parents, John and Donna were more strict in the beginning, especially with the first three children. They've mellowed a bit since. The house is also a bed and breakfast now, since Mitch went off to college, so it isn't just home to the family anymore. Strangers come and go, bringing with them pieces of other lives. They've also played host to a series of children from Thailand. The children grew up with chores, some in the kitchen, some in the house, some in the barn.

"I learned discipline at a real young age," Mitch says. "You blinked wrong and you paid the consequences. You had to ask if you could have an apple, you couldn't just take it. The older kids in my family call it the Infamous Eighties. We weren't allowed to watch TV except on Sunday, when we could watch football. That's changed, since our parents started the B&B; they have four TV sets now, and a VCR. We tell the younger four that they have it much easier than we did. But growing up that way taught me a lot about the work ethic."

The family raised a bull for meat once, when Mitch was a boy. The farmer who gave them the calf warned them not to think of him as a pet, so they didn't really name him. They called him Bull, and couldn't help feeling something for him. Once, when Bull caught pneumonia and almost died, the oldest children helped nurse him back to health. When they eventually had Bull slaughtered, Mitch refused to eat his meat.

The Clarks were not inclined to drive their children into town every other hour. They encouraged the brood to become friends among themselves instead, to the point where even now the seven talk a great deal across the miles, and share their secrets. Because his brother Johnny was five years younger, and there were few neighbors, Mitch entertained himself in ways that helped his imagination grow. One of his favorite stories is about his football games. Alone in his side yard, he was the team, the coach, the referee, the radio commentator. He was quarterback and receiver on a play. "I have an incredible imagination now," he says. "I was never bored." And his ability to see what other people couldn't would come in handy years later.

I actually think imagination runs in the family. Many times over the years, first as a student and then as a journalist, I called upon Mitch's dad for thoughts about the depths of sport beyond what I saw on the playing field. John just thought more about what athletics meant in the big picture, the ways that athletes think and how an athlete's sport connected to the rest of his or her life. He designed press guides and posters, using his own artistic abilities and calling upon wrestlers who could draw. John valued versatility. Most of St. Lawrence's upper weights were football players during the fall, and John took pride in recruiting young men who could excel at both sports. He was a promoter. When he flew to California for the 1976 NCAA Division III tournament with Ron Pelligra, our senior heavyweight who that year became our first national champion, John arranged a photo shoot in Palm Springs with movie star Kirk Douglas, a 1939 graduate who had wrestled for St. Lawrence. He's the father of movie star Michael Douglas. The pictures from that day, of Pelligra "wrestling" Douglas, ran in the Syracuse papers and are still classics in our archives. Mitch supplied the drive and determination for his wrestling career and his mom saw to his spiritual side, providing a depth of feeling and humility. But the rest of the vision behind what he achieved came from John.

Concerned about the atmosphere and cultural influences in public school, the Clarks sent their older children to Bible school at first. Mitch went to the Bible school through fifth grade, when he shifted with the others to Canton schools. He was a mouthy kid, often in detention, and whenever he was kept after school his father would whip him with a belt. John was tougher on his oldest boy, thinking that was the way to raise him. John was, at least in my memory, probably a more stern coach of his college wrestling team at that time than he was later. His thinking broadened and his tolerance grew with the years. It happens when you get older.

The Clarks were about more than just sports. They encouraged their children to spend time outdoors, in the wilderness. Years later, climbing hills and carrying logs became a crucial part of Mitch's training. They bought a camp nearby on Trout Lake and moved the family there during the summer. They went hiking and canoeing; John liked to use mountain hikes as a bonding tool for his college wrestlers. John became an accomplished fly fisherman; for several years, he was involved in a PBS television show about fishing that is syndicated on 200 stations across the U.S. and Canada. Donna managed the household and became a baker capable of making batches of bagels and muffins for her brood.

The Clarks valued academics, though they stressed this more with their daughters. They did not push Mitch to excel as a student beyond what he could, and sometimes they're surprised that they didn't. So is Mitch. As a St. Lawrence University student, Donna was Phi Beta Kappa, the highest honor society, but as a parent she hesitated to stress schoolwork too much with her children because she found it an empty pursuit in and of itself. "I wanted to succeed in academics because I didn't feel I was good in other things," she says. She and John were more intent on having their children pursue excellence in other ways in school, such as citizenship.

And they made God part of their family. They had Bible study every Wednesday and devotions every night. Donna and John became the pastors of a non-denominational Christian church. John helped by managing such things as the weekly program and announcements, while Donna gave the sermons. Donna attributes part of Mitch's drive to succeed in wrestling to his spirituality. In an essay written when he was in elementary school, Mitch says he wanted to be a missionary, to save people in Africa and Russia. Mitch now says that he was force-fed religion as a boy and didn't know any differently, and later swore he'd never do the same to his children. But he is grateful for what he has gained from his spiritual side. He has accepted faith as part of his life at times and rejected it at others, but ultimately he has turned to it in times of crisis and believes it's played a crucial role in his success.

Mitch's parents tried to impress upon him that he should be modest no matter what he accomplished. He says he struggled to be humble, knowing he was special "but not too cocky about it."

"Mom always said, 'Pride goeth before a fall,' and I'd say, 'Good, that means I'll get a pin sometime soon,' " Mitch says (fall being another word for pin, for anyone new to wrestling). John was stern but Donna, more behind the scenes than her husband when it came to sports, could be just as steely in her resolve that their children be obedient, hard-working and humble about whatever they did. Donna and John guided them loosely in other ways. "They weren't into counseling, they were more likely to say, 'You'll figure out how to do it,' " he says. "A fend-for-yourself attitude."

Mitch doesn't remember a time when he didn't wrestle. His father took him to peewee tournaments as soon as he was old enough. Over the years Mitch would hang around the practice room where his father's St. Lawrence teams worked out. In the summer he was around during SLU's wrestling camp, where one of the chief teachers each summer was Russ Hellickson.

For the Clark girls, sports has been important — they've succeeded in swimming and soccer — but it's more of a social outlet and a way to stay in shape than a central pillar of their lives. For the boys, it's been a different matter. Wrestling ruled the family's winters. John Clark didn't know as much about those other sports, and wrestling was such a part of him that he poured his soul into it. At times the sisters were jealous, Mitch says, especially when he was at Ohio State and his parents would fly out to see him wrestle but not visit his older sisters a few hours from them in New York State as much as Christy and Nicki would've liked. But they made peace with it.

John Clark believes that champion wrestlers must be built, using a system and bringing the focus of the wrestler's life into a certain pattern about six weeks before a major championship. He thinks a wrestler's life has certain pieces to it, and that all of them must work or his drive for a title, except in the rarest cases, will collapse. He tried his system first on Mitch.

Wrestling Takes the Little Boy
Out of You

(Mitch)

My parents started me out in wrestling when I was a small boy, so I don't remember a time when I wasn't learning to be at home on the mat. Dad coached the sport every winter, taught

Mitch "takes top" for the first time

it every summer at wrestling camp, and thought about recruiting or how to guide his wrestlers with their lives, if they asked, the rest of the time. He must have been overjoyed to have a son, and to have one who liked wrestling, because I did like it. He took me to peewee tournaments when I was a skinny little wisp of a kid, and he was at the mat's edge throughout my high school career.

Dad says I always did better than people expected me to, from those early years on. Because I was John Clark's son, and wrestling is a small world in Northern New York, people watched me a bit more. I got used to it. I was a competitor, something that's pretty hard to teach anybody.

"When you were little, I used to get on the living room carpet and you had to pin me with your chest," Dad says. "It was miraculous that I did it, since that ended up being the finish of your best move, the half nelson. So you learned at a young age to make little adjustments, to close in on a guy like a python wrapping somebody up."

You must love competition. It's not important whom you wrestle, your biggest opponent wears your uniform. You must overcome your own shortcomings.

I once told Dad that I didn't care what the score was, I could still win.

I also told him once that the last minute of any match is mine.

One day in seventh grade, aching in mind and body from what I'd confronted about myself, I told him, "Wrestling takes the little boy out of you."

I spent six years on the varsity. I was lucky to live in New York, one of the few states that allow someone to be varsity in seventh and eighth grades, if he or she passes certain physical maturity tests. For four of those years, I was a sectional champion, meaning I qualified for the state tournament. In New York, only the winner of each weight class in each of the 13 sections advances to the state tournament, and there's only one tournament. Many sections have their own class tournaments, for schools of different sizes, but they all have an overall sectional tournament. There's been talk in recent years of having three state tournaments, but I hope it never happens. Since our tournament started in 1963, it's always brought together wrestlers from all kinds of schools. In any weight class, the champion might come from some big suburban school, or a tiny school in the middle of cow country, or (rarely) a city school. So many times, one finalist in a state title bout comes from crowded, suburban Long Island, where the only way you know you're driving from one town to another is because a sign says so, and the other finalist comes from a village near the Adirondacks or on the Pennsylvania border. Our state tournament was such a great event.

I'm sure most state tournaments are the same, but to the high school wrestler, it's like the Olympics every time you step on a mat in front of all those people. New York State's tournament has been at the Onondaga

County War Memorial in downtown Syracuse, almost the center of the state, since the early 1970s. The place has been home to professional hockey over the years, and basketball, and things like circuses, concerts, professional wrestling, boxing and conventions. It's enormous, with a curved ceiling, a central area surrounded by the boards of a hockey rink, and room for four mats end-to-end, with seating for wrestlers and coaches on one side and for the officials and press on the other. There are two main levels of seats. Parents and boosters hang banners up near the roof, telling everyone how great a certain kid is or a certain school.

The tournament begins Friday afternoon with a parade of all the sectional champions, by section. It ends with a parade of finalists to the center mat. For two days it's just pandemonium. You hear cheers in bursts from this spot, then that spot. The little dramas just stretch on. For years the two Long Island sections dominated; wrestling is ingrained in their culture, in those suburbs sprawling east from New York City. Gradually other sections took turns winning the overall team title. Mine never came close. It was cause for celebration when we had a state semifinalist or state finalist, I suppose, though I never saw one. Seeing that place, when I'd go there with Dad, before I ever went there as a sectional champion, I wanted to be the first from my section to stand up on that center mat with hands raised in triumph.

Never did my father have to tell me to work out, even when I had to get up early and run. I'm not a morning person by any means, but wrestling made me one at times during the season. The motivation was there. When I was in 10th grade, I placed fourth in the state but I knew I was out of shape and I began to run more. Stamina can win more matches than technique or strength can. Over the years, when American wrestlers beat Russians in close bouts, it was because American wrestlers relied on stamina while Russians relied on practicing technique until it was perfect. I'm not the most coordinated or fastest wrestler you ever saw, so I have to rely on other things, and being in shape is one of them.

Dad believes that champion wrestlers are made by planning their seasons and careers around a framework of eight building blocks: diet and nutrition, conditioning, technique, weight training, mental preparation, drilling and natural talent (genes). If any of these fail or you neglect them, the whole framework collapses. In teaching me to be a champion, he planned my approach to each of these building blocks. Later he planned

Johnny's training around them, and I'm sure he'll do the same for Charlie, the youngest.

Dad was accustomed to coaching college-age men at St. Lawrence. I was his first son, and anybody who is an oldest child knows what it can be like to be the first child in anything. Young parents learn on the older children, starting with the oldest. In me, Dad saw a guy who lacked much ability but made up for it with determination. So he molded me, and it wasn't always easy for either of us.

I could be pretty rebellious. Before ninth grade I used to mouth off a lot. I'd overreact to losses, and after wins I might say, "Big deal." Once, after winning a match, I twirled my finger as if to say, "La-dee-da." My parents were furious. After a loss in sixth grade, I threw my headgear. After Dad was done with me, I never did it again. He was very strict, he wanted perfection, I think he compared me to his college wrestlers. If I did a stand-up technique the wrong way, I'd get hit in the back of the head and yelled at. I'd be crying, "I'm trying!" I don't fault him for being tough on me — actually, we were two competitive people, knocking heads. I once stood chin-to-chin with him, fists clenched, ready for action. Nothing came of it, though. Once, in eighth grade, I thought I could dust him in a match. Three minutes later I was pinned, with a bloody nose and mouth.

Wrestling was Dad's domain. Once, when Mom wondered about my losing weight, he said, "Donna, I don't tell you how to cook, you don't tell me how to coach Mitch."

You could compare a national champion to a person who climbs to a mountain's highest spot, like those people who are always trying to reach Mt. Everest's summit. These people need the help of many others to make it. It starts out as a large expedition, helped by guides. They camp at one spot, reach a higher spot and camp there. They gauge the best path to the top, find their way through obstacles, and finally fewer of them push on to the next-highest spot on the peak. And the last climber or climbers go on to the top. Every champion athlete is like that mountain climber: the product of many people who push him and plot his course. In my case, my parents were the managers of that expedition, but many other people helped. They pushed, they coaxed, they taught me. Then they fell back and let me go on.

Every wrestling team has guys who run the show and let the younger guys know it. They put the younger guys, especially the new ones, through a period of proving who they are. I think it's human nature. I see it especially with boys and young men, up through college age. Canton's varsity had a few such guys, two of them named Jason Crosby and Jeremy Filiatrault, and they made it a point to beat on me. They said they wanted to make me tougher. I think they succeeded.

Three or four of them used to pin me down and just pound me. It sounds cruel, and maybe it was, a little, but it's part of belonging to a team. I guess they saw a skinny kid who needed to learn to suck it up mentally, and they decided this was the way to do it. We would spend weekend nights working out and planning how to get better, instead of going out and partying or succumbing to the other pressures that confront high school students.

You have to endure it. You won't get anywhere by crying about it or complaining to the coach (unless it really gets out of line). You're going to face so many problems in life, and some of them will get easier as you get older, but new problems will replace them. One of those guys used to hold a cigarette lighter's flame under kids' arms, seeing how much pain they could take. I think he'd seen too many movies. But I put up with it, and I got tougher. My only regret is that as I got older, and bigger, I had to wrestle off against some of those guys to see who would be in the lineup. Not all of them could be. But I owe them so much. Jason and Jeremy graduated from high school two years ahead of me, and when I went off to college, they told me they were hurt that I never cited them in newspaper interviews after they'd left. Know what? They were right, and I regret that, but it's often hard to thank everyone for helping you to get where you got. My advice to younger athletes is to give credit where it's deserved. It always means a lot to those who supported you.

I owe a lot to the wrestlers on my father's St. Lawrence teams, too.

I grew up idolizing some of those guys, who were going through manhood while I was still a pup. There's nothing quite like having an older athlete to look up to. Every high school athlete should have one or two. I had many of them, because Dad had built his program into a national contender, so he had All-Americans left and right. There was Mark Shortsleeve, who had transferred to SLU after wrestling for Nebraska and then for New York's Brockport State, one of the top Division

III programs. Mark was from Fulton, Dad's hometown, and he'd placed second in the state in high school. He became a national champion at St. Lawrence in 1986, at 134 pounds. He stuck around as an assistant coach. He used to work with me, push me. Mark was very close to our family, so he'd be around when Dad and I bumped heads. He was the mediator, and he taught me a lot about discipline. I don't think I've seen him for five years, and he probably has no idea how much of an influence he had on me.

There were a batch of guys, each of them with his own wisdom to pass to a kid. They were my heroes, and then they graduated and became lawyers, businessmen, teachers.

One particular SLU wrestler who had a major influence on me was Wess Audsley, Class of 1981, who started at heavyweight. Wess was a counselor at the SLU summer camp and later, as a doctoral student at Ohio State, practiced with the Buckeyes. He'd met Coach Russ Hellickson at the SLU camp. Over the years Wess finished his doctoral studies in sports management and went to work for a sports marketing firm. A man of dry wit and patience, and enormous physical power, he became my friend as I grew into a teenager and, through his encouragement, spent part of every summer at Ohio State's Buckeye Wrestling Camp. He showed me international wrestling's upper reaches, first at a U.S.-Russia dual meet that his firm set up in 1990, then through a Grand Prix tournament, a pre-Olympic event, that his firm put together at Ohio State two years later. Some of my high school teammates and I would go the Buckeye camp, and we learned about the intensity of a Division I athlete very quickly. Wess would push us through weight lifting and drilling sessions, and make us run the infamous stairs of Ohio Stadium.

The next step in my journey, after learning the basics and getting to feel at home, was to reach my high school's varsity team. I did it as a seventh grader. I had to wait for the next step, though — the sectional title. I lost in the sectional finals in both seventh and eighth grades to a guy named Willy Dumas, from Malone, a village north of us. The first time was at 91 pounds, the next time was at 105 pounds. Dumas just countered everything I threw at him. I'd start a move, he'd finish it. Dad remembers wondering, as he watched this, if I'd ever amount to anything as a wrestler. He didn't tell me that. I just kept working.

Two things happened in those early years on the varsity that taught me self-confidence. They were the kind of moments that transform your life, the kind you will always remember.

One day in eighth grade, I went camping in the Adirondack Mountains with two college students. I thought we were just going for a hike, but it turned out to be much more. I ended up risking my life, or at least my health. We climbed Mt. Colden, going up an incline instead of taking a trail that most hikers took. We got onto an icy ledge on the mountain's face, on a steep slope that had water trickling down it. We should've used ropes, but we didn't; we climbed using our feet and hands. Ultimately, if we'd have slipped, we would have slid for 50 feet and then off a cliff. We made it, applauded by people who had climbed the mountain on the trail side.

Those two students were simply adrenaline junkies.

Not long afterward, two people died climbing that same slope.

What we did wasn't my style, but I did it. I don't shy away from challenges.

The other event was a wrestling match in ninth grade. First, I lost by technical fall to a senior from a different section south of mine. After that match my father said maybe I wasn't cut out for wrestling. The senior's name was Chris Lynch. He would go on to be a sectional champion from his area that year. He was a stud. But two weeks after he humiliated me, I beat him in the finals of a tournament and earned the Outstanding Wrestler trophy.

Every wrestler has a defining match, a bout that serves as a turning point in his career. You're never the same after that day. The match against Chris Lynch was mine. It marked the beginning of my goal to be a state champion, the first one from my section. We'd come close in the past, with state runners-up in 1973, 1980 and 1985 (all of which I knew as ancient history), but we had yet to see one of our own stand there in the center of the Onondaga County War Memorial in Syracuse, with his hand raised before the crowd, in first place.

The state title became my dream of dreams in ninth grade, when I reached the state tournament as a 132-pounder. I didn't place, but getting there was a step.

As a sophomore I placed fourth at 145 pounds, after losing in overtime in the semifinals. My high school team's coach, Neal Riggs, thought it was astonishing that I reached the semifinals. "It was a difference of strength in that semifinal bout," he says. "It was a sophomore against a senior. If you'd hung on, you'd have been a finalist."

Taking fourth was a step, too, but my father began to think I'd grown as much as I could against competition in my section. The section had some tough kids, but not enough of them to push each other to that next level. Dad began to look for other ways to find the kind of competition that would force me to grow into a wrestler who would have a shot at a state title. He asked a club south of us, in the area around Syracuse and Utica, if I could join. He would drive me down there, a three-hour trip under ideal weather and often longer in the winter, when snow blasts off Lake Ontario and causes whiteouts, to practice with this club. But the club said no, though its directors said they wanted me for their traveling team. Dad said no thanks, and looked in another direction.

People in the north speculated that my parents would send me to preparatory school, as so many parents sent their children to prep school to grow as athletes and at the same time gain better academic habits. My father had spent a year at prep school after graduating from high school. The newspapers also speculated that I might live with Dad's relatives in Fulton and go to school there, to become part of a great team on the state level. But that wasn't a serious thought.

No, Dad and I found our solution about two hours northeast of Canton, in Montreal.

Against "Man Strength"

(Mitch)

Throughout this book I continuously stress the importance of hard work and sacrifice. I'm sure you have heard it before, but as Russ Hellickson always says, "The key to being successful is hard work and learning how to get mentally tougher." With that said, I want to admit to you that I wasn't always gung-ho or mentally stable. There have been many days when I felt like a slug and my laziness would get the best of me. That is human nature. Wrestling season can drag on and take a lot out of you. After the season you should take a good break and get back into it when your mind and body tell you they're ready.

In the off-season I tried to at least once a day do something that would benefit my wrestling for the coming season. It might've been a sprint workout, or a couple of live wrestling matches, or a lifting session. Doubling up some of these workouts into two a day will only help you. It will keep you focused on your goal or goals and add to your confidence.

Jim Jordan, two-time national champion at the University of Wisconsin and now a congressman from Ohio, has a quote that every serious wrestler should remember: "The amount of confidence you have is directly proportional to how hard you have worked."

Anybody who wrestles must at some point face an opponent twice his size, someone who is bigger, taller, stronger. Coaches tend to mismatch guys in the practice room to give a wrestler the chance to test whatever he has against an opponent far heavier and more powerful. That was the idea behind my trips to the freestyle club in Montreal, two hours away.

Dad had for many years taken his St. Lawrence University teams to compete in the Montreal Open, early in the college season, as a sort of prelude to its own opponents. There he met Dr. Victor Zilberman, a Russian who was a three-time Soviet National Champion and then left his homeland and settled in Canada. He was now the Canadian national coach for the 1988, 1992 and 1996 Olympic teams. Dad asked if I could work out with the club, which was in a YMCA then and is now in a private high school. Victor said yes.

Two or three times a week, my junior and senior years in high school, Dad drove me to that club, north from Canton to Massena, New York, then along the St. Lawrence River's south shore to the bridge across to Cornwall, Ontario, then northeast along the Queen Elizabeth Way (a major highway) into the Province of Quebec, to the city of Montreal. He molded his work schedule around it. To Dad, this was my chance to push myself beyond my league.

It was a huge sacrifice for my father, who had to worry about the other athletic teams at St. Lawrence. It really wore him out. In fact, one night he fell asleep at the wheel while driving home from Montreal. We ended up in a ditch, neither of us injured by some stroke of luck.

At the club I pitted my teenager's skills and physique against guys who were 25, 26, 30 and who were Canadian national champions and Olympic medal contenders. They had what we call "man strength."

At that time the club was on the second floor of an old YMCA, in a place used as a nursery school during the day. Sometimes I'd notice the contrast: Olympic-caliber athletes grimly working out while next to the mat sat nursery toys, plastic slides, miniature houses. I'd get angry and hit a toy or something. It was strange in that sense, because the atmosphere in that room was so businesslike.

I made an impression on Victor early by speaking my mind, as Americans do. Dad likes to remind me of the day I threw my headgear out of frustration and Victor told me to pick it up because "you can't do that here." He said, "Meetch, you've got to learn to control your emotions before you control your opponent." When I said something, the others always looked at me funny, because I was the first person to come in and mouth off to him.

Both men and women were welcome at this club. So were teens and younger guys. I never knew who I was going to find there when we made the drive each time. I used to work out with a couple of Turks and a Swede, both superb freestyle wrestlers. There were Iranians. Several of the guys who practiced at the club were Russians who, like Victor, had fled their home countries and settled in Canada. They had names like Oleg Ladik, Gia Sissaouri, Kakha and Zaza Verkhviachvili. They were heroes back home, some of them among the best in the world at their sport, and in Montreal they had to accept menial jobs and scramble for money. The summer before I left for Ohio State, I went on a European tour with them, and I mainly found out the meager life for people in what we know as the former Soviet Union. My father used to bring the guys small gifts because he felt badly for the way they had to adapt to a friendlier but more expensive environment.

I didn't score a point on any of them for the first three months.

Then, gradually, I began to hold my own.

I won a match, then a few more, then about half of my matches.

Victor ran the practice sessions as absolute master, showing his displeasure with the way you were wrestling but rarely complementing anyone. Warm-fuzzy is not the Russian way. In fact, revealing one's emotions is not the Russian way. You train by doing the same thing over and over. You don't change gears, just stay at one even pace, honing the same technique day in and day out, perfectly executed but not too intense. People ask me about the culture of that practice room, what it was like to be among them, but to me it was just a matter of going in there and getting out of there. Do your workouts and go home.

Victor always saw something in me, that I had a chance to be a world champion at freestyle. My father and I don't know to this day why he decided this, but when I was a senior in high school he began to tell Dad that I should not go to college, I should move to Montreal and train with him. My parents were also discussing at the time whether to send me to prep school for another year, before college.

"Victor was very frustrated," Dad says. "He would say to me, 'John, if Mitch was a gymnast or figure skater, you'd do it, but he's a wrestler.' We argued about it."

In the end, both Montreal and the prep school ideas were shelved. There's no doubt that those practices against those men, against man strength, did much to shape me and push me along the path toward my national championship. But in the end, I went to college.

Chapter Five

Dropping Pounds

(Mitch)

This is as good a time as any to talk about losing weight. In a way, it's like talking about two different sports: wrestling before 1997, when our sport became the talk of the nation for the wrong reason, and wrestling after 1997, when the rules for weight loss changed. It's also like talking about two different sports because the process of losing weight is so all-inclusive and demanding that it could be another sport unto itself. There are great wrestlers who are good at shedding pounds and some who are not, and there are wrestlers who have made themselves better because they knew how to do it—because losing pounds the wrong way can weaken you and cause you not to reach your potential.

Most wrestlers have to shed at least some pounds to reach their ideal weight class. You spend the beginning of the week before a weekend match training for it, then during the second half of the week you focus on making the weight. Then, once that's done, you mentally prepare for competition. You do this week after week for five months. That's why wrestling is the hardest sport on your mind and body, bar none.

Parents and nutritionists worried about weight loss in wrestling long before the fall of 1997 when three college wrestlers, Billy Saylor of Campbell, Joe LaRosa of Wisconsin-LaCrosse and Jeff Reese of Michigan, died from trying to drop too many pounds too quickly. Weight loss was (and is) part of the sport's discipline. A team might have two or three guys at one weight class, and need someone to drop down to fill another weight class, and that guy begins to plan how he'll do it without getting too weak. It's amazing to see a wrestler in the school cafeteria, eating a few leaves of lettuce or eating nothing while, all around him, kids scarf up chips, burgers, french fries, all the things they take for granted as part of lunch. The same scene takes place later, at home, when the rest of the family is gulping down dinner while the son or sons who wrestle drink some water and munch on granola. And when people hesitate to eat in front of you, you need to be tough and say no, go ahead, it's no big deal. That's heavy stuff for a teenaged guy to handle.

When you made weight, it was such a great feeling because doing it was so hard on your body and spirit. Not always, of course. My father said that he enjoyed the feeling he had while cutting weight. All of your senses are heightened, you smell and taste things in a different way. He believes that you are sharper mentally and physically during this time. I agree to a point, but once you have cut the final ounces and are hours away from weigh-ins, I believe that period of time is a different story. That's when you are struggling and you become focused just on getting on the scales.

What I did to lose weight I wouldn't want my son to do. My college teammate Dan DiCesare and I used to tell each other that. "No way is my son going to do this." Dan was dropping to 150, I was dropping to 177 — about 20 pounds. For the NCAA championship bout, when I was a junior, I actually weighed 203.

There were times in college when I'd be so dizzy from weight loss that I'd walk 10 feet, sit down, walk 10 feet, sit down. I saw times when maybe people could have died, as those three college wrestlers died. I remember times when I'd drink water after making weight, and lie there, deathly ill, waiting for my body to absorb that water.

I can't blame a guy for losing weight for his sport. Our society is always encouraging people to take short cuts, to win at all costs. With the new rules to determine weight class and pre-competition weigh-ins, some guys won't win as much now. Before this change, they won because they were good weight cutters. But now they can't get down to a lower weight class anymore. I guess it's a moot point.

As an eighth grader I wanted to drop from 112 to 105 pounds. My parents said no. I fought with them every day until they relented after I wrote a diet plan showing how I'd do it for the sectional tournament. The plan called for granola in the morning, a lunch of a tuna sandwich and an EXCEED shake, and dinner of a salad, for seven days. I followed it until the seventh day, when I didn't eat at all. I was so skinny. That last night, I cried myself to sleep. I was so thin and had no energy, and I was scared. The next day, on the way to the sectional tournament, Dad said, "If you

don't win this tournament, I'll still be proud of you for sticking with it."
When my sister Christy saw me, an hour after weigh-ins, she cried.

I took second to my nemesis from Malone, Willy Dumas, but I'd
achieved something else. I'd lost the weight.

Still, losing that weight might have cost me. I had profuse nose bleeds
every match, and I believe it had an effect on my performance against
Dumas, because I had beaten on him two weeks earlier at a higher weight.

You diet so incredibly hard. You feel such animosity for people who
eat normally. You see them waste food, or eat but not enjoy it. And you
find yourself disliking people who are overweight; you can't understand
how they could be that way.

Once, in ninth grade, I tried something stupid. I put on a winter hat, a
couple of layers of clothing and a couple of blankets, including an electric blanket. I turned the electric blanket up high and went to sleep. When
I woke up, I was in my underwear. I'd undressed while half-asleep, as if
my body knew it was overheating and saved itself. I might've died.

I've also heard of guys keeping their windows open in the middle of
winter, to shiver the weight off while sleeping. I guess stories like those
give wrestling a bad name.

Water was the worst thing. It was so much easier to go without eating
than to go without drinking water. I'd lose so much weight, I'd see my
face sinking in, feel my hands getting thinner. If I drove past a body of
water, like a pond or lake, I'd think that I could drink the whole thing —
and truly believe it.

Then, of course, after weighing in at the match, I'd drink two cups and
feel like throwing up because it seemed like so much.

People in school didn't understand, which upset me. My peers, teachers, other kids' parents — they'd yell at me, things like "Why are you
doing this? You look awful. Why do this to your body?" That made the
whole experience harder. I wanted to be praised for showing the will
power to do it, not chastised.

Not to mention that weight loss is time consuming. While other students were out doing what young people do, having fun, I'd be in a sauna,
riding a stationary bike, doing what I had to.

To lose weight, I did more than eat less. I worked out, which burns
more fat than anything. I worked out before school. I used to run, sometimes when it was dark and minus 40 degrees, breathing through a scarf,

not hearing the snowplow until it was almost on top of me. Somehow I always made it by the end of the week, no matter how high my weight was, as if my body knew what it had to do from Sunday to Friday.

Losing weight was always one more bond among wrestlers, something that we understood about our sport that outsiders might not grasp. There are so many times in wrestling when you feel alone, or wonder why you're doing this, and getting rid of those pounds is one of those times. Other wrestlers understand that. It's one of the reasons we're so close.

American society just doesn't grasp the feeling of trying to lose that last pound. But you feel so good that you pushed your body in so many ways: against a practice partner, against food, against a wall that you pushed through. Your confidence grows so much from such times. Russ told me once that 99.9 percent of the population has never needed to use the discipline or feel the pains from cutting weight that we felt.

Question from a parent: I worry about what weight loss will do to growing boys. What are your thoughts?

I say don't let them lose weight by starving themselves. Starving yourself slows your metabolism, which means you won't practice and train as well. It's better to eat five or six small meals a day, and exercise. That speeds up your metabolism.

Losing weight didn't stunt my growth. It might even have triggered my growth spurts. I grew from 91 pounds in seventh grade to 105 (eighth grade), to 132 (ninth), to 145 (10th), to 155 (11th) and finally to 167 (senior year). Actually, I wrestled at least one match at every high school weight class. I can't say that it stunted my height — I'm 6'3" tall.

So Close to the Goal

(Mitch)

The dream started in ninth grade, when I won a bout at the state tournament, and it intensified in 10th grade, when I placed fourth. I wanted to be the first state champion from my section.

I believed it was possible.

Things like league champion and regional champion are the kind of achievements people in your town remember for years. Plenty of athletes don't achieve that level. State champion? That's huge, like being a legend. The word "legend" is used an awful lot in sports, but it applies; people talk about you all over town for the rest of your life. National champion? Only a few high school athletes think about something so far up there, it's hard to picture.

I didn't think much about national honors. To a kid from St. Lawrence County, a state title in wrestling was dream enough.

By the time I was in 11th grade, I'd pushed to a new level of intensity about wrestling. Dad began driving me to Montreal two to three times a week to practice against men, but other things were happening to make me stronger.

Wess Audsley, St. Lawrence University's heavyweight in the Class of 1981, who was studying for his doctorate in sports management at Ohio State, had convinced a few of us Canton boys to come to Ohio State wrestling camp, to get out of New York. It was Wess who dreamed up ways for me to build up my skinny body, ways you won't find in your local gym. He thought of ways to work out that were fun, suited my body type and were unusual enough to appeal to me.

We pushed a car.

Specifically, we pushed his Jeep around a parking lot at Ohio State. I'd push it a ways and he'd push it back. When I got home, I kept pushing cars.

Car pushing

It's simple, really. Put a car in neutral and brace yourself behind it. Lean right into the bumper and the back section. Use your legs. Ask someone to steer, either walking next to it or, if the person is light enough, in the driver's seat. Then clock whoever is pushing. See how fast you can move the car from point to point.

Feel the way your muscles burn afterward, in your legs and back and shoulders. As anyone who lifts weights can tell you, when your muscles are burning, they're rebuilding themselves — stronger.

At home in the country, I put a car on the road in front of our house and pushed it for distances I measured using telephone poles. The poles were maybe 50 to 75 yards apart. I'd push the car for two poles, then Johnny would push it back while I steered. Next we would switch places and do it all over again. I used to get sick for about 15 minutes after these workouts, as if I'd been hit by a semi truck.

I often didn't tell my family about my training methods. At our summer home, I'd head off into the hills to run, or do something else that was out of the ordinary. Then I'd be sweating later, breathing hard, and my family would wonder what I'd been doing. I didn't mention the car pushing. Dad looked out the front window one day and saw my car going down the road, slowly, without a driver. He thought it was odd. Then he saw the car come back. He finally found out what I was up to.

The summer before my senior year my parents added a clay tennis court at our summer home on Trout Lake. My mother encouraged me to take lessons, and I usually replied, "I'm trying to train to win a national championship." Actually I just had mixed feelings about picking up tennis, knowing I would probably lose to my mother, who had more experience with the sport. Eventually I agreed to try it, and played all summer. I found it increased my foot speed and helped me keep an aerobic base. By the end of the summer Johnny and I would battle under the hot son, Johnny of course beating me every time.

Moving sand

Another alternative form of working out came through moving sand. I literally was responsible for making a beach volleyball court at our summer home. Shoveling sand into a wheelbarrow and trudging with it through sand is an excellent way to build up your legs and back.

I often would start the day by rowing our four-seat boat down the 1.5 mile-long lake. I would pull the oars (using lats and biceps) on the way down and push them (using chest and triceps) on the way back.

Mountain climbing was a great way to build my legs and hips. The Adirondacks have trails that didn't require ropes to climb but were steep enough to totally exhaust my legs and burn my lungs for three to five miles.

Construction was done near our summer home that involved dynamite to break up rock. My father and I would bring home flat but very heavy rocks used for stepping stones. I found it to be a really good work-

Chapter Six

Rowing a canoe on Trout Lake

out, especially for my lower back and hamstrings. The only problem was, I knew if I dropped one on my foot I could miss my senior season. Sure enough, one day I did exactly that, and the moment the rock landed on my foot I screamed in pain. I grabbed the nearest thing I could, which was a tree a little taller than myself. To my surprise I instantly pulled it out of the ground with ease. The interesting thing about it is, after I calmed down I decided to pull out another tree half the size of the first one, and it didn't budge. The only reason I mention this is, it just goes to show how effective adrenaline or focused energy can be. Once you are able to concentrate and direct the flow of adrenaline for certain lengths of time, you can reach The Zone.

Alternative training methods such as these allowed me to train without the risk of boredom or burnout. Again, my imagination was a tool toward my success in wrestling.

Wess Audsley has been one of the main figures in my life ever since, a friend and mentor who knows so much about sports and life. He worked for a sports marketing firm in Columbus for much of the time I was at Ohio State, and often I'd hang out at his house, getting his take on things. He and his wife, Joanne, have been good to me. They moved to Western New York a few years ago when Wess became the Batavia YMCA's executive director, but I stop in to see them when I can.

Wess and I became friends at the same time, as much as a 30-year-old and a 15-year-old can be. I'd always been this little kid hanging around the practice room when he was in college, and he saw me grow up. He's been there for some of the best moments of my life.

As I said at the beginning, a wrestler is the product of several coaches. Along with my father, and at times Wess, I could call upon my high school coach, Neal Riggs. Coach Riggs had been guiding Canton teams since 1968, when he'd come north to teach physical education after graduating from Ithaca College, which has one of the more successful athletic programs in college sports at any level (as in three NCAA Division III national champions each in wrestling and football, two each in baseball and women's soccer). He'd grown up in Ithaca, New York, the small city that is home to Ithaca College and Cornell University. It's about 30 miles from the Pennsylvania border, a cosmopolitan little place with a blue-collar side to it. Wrestling's roots run deep there. Before New York had a state tournament, the only way schools could judge their power in our sport was to travel to each other for dual meets, or have meets between two sections. Ithaca High School regularly dominated these dual meets. That was the heritage for Coach Riggs and his teammates in the 1960s.

Coach Riggs is one of those men who know how to talk to high school guys. He knows how to motivate, how to find out what's eating you. He's one of those rare adults who relate to you in such a way that you know he understands what it's like to be a teenager. He still likes teenagers as much as he did when he began teaching. He respects a high school student's world, and you respect him for it. Another positive influence on me was our health teacher and assistant coach, Abe Brafman. Abe loved the sport of wrestling; however, his biggest impact on me was off the mat. His advice helped me mature through those awkward teenage years of growing up.

It was probably inevitable that Coach Riggs and my dad clashed as my coaches. During my bouts, each of them would yell instructions to me. Sometimes their commands conflicted. Dad finally agreed, when I was in 10th grade, that Coach Riggs should be the one to yell to me. But Dad was still very much there when I wrestled, photographing me from the side of the mat or watching from the front of the bleachers.

Luckily, Dad and Coach Riggs became good friends and learned to work together. That was important, because too often parents try so hard to support their athlete kid that they interfere, cause tensions, become counterproductive. Even when the parent is a coach, or at least a very knowledgable person, somehow he or she has to work out a partnership with the coaches.

I entered the 1992 state tournament as a junior with the determination to reach my goal of a championship. I was a dark horse at 155 pounds, not expected to win, and it helped.

For some reason I've always worried about every opponent (a trait my brother Johnny shares). In a tournament situation, I'm always nervous at the beginning and relax as I advance through a tournament.

The thing about tournaments is, no matter how close you are to your teammates, you must concentrate on yourself. In the case of a championship tournament, like the state meet or the NCAA, this is more true. Sure, there's a team title on the line, but you must focus on how you are doing.

At major tournaments, I try not to watch other people wrestle, because it just distracts me from my purpose. I would tell anyone else to do the same.

I'd add this:

> Don't stand all day. Sit. Rest for your bouts.
> Don't spend much time watching your teammates compete. It could take the mental edge from you. You'll find out soon enough how they did. If you get into every one of their matches, you too will burn more energy and will be tired for your own matches.

In this situation, I felt no pressure. Everyone knew who the favorite was in my weight class: Jason Kraft of Sachem High School on Long Island, one of the biggest high schools in the state. I was a kid from a section that had never produced a state champion. The Syracuse newspapers noted me as a contender at 155, but Kraft was the man. He went on to wrestle at the University of Nebraska.

As much as I recall the final bout, I recall the semifinal that I won to get there. How often do you have to go to another location for a state semifinal, riding in a police paddy wagon?

In two weight classes that year, the champions from the section that stretches from Albany to the southern Adirondack towns were quarantined. They were from Glens Falls, a small city about 45 minutes north of Albany, on the lip of the Adirondacks. Measles had been diagnosed among students in the Glens Falls schools. New York's health officials were strict about measles; everyone who could be exposed needed to be vaccinated. In the case of a sports team from a school that had suffered a measles outbreak, the game or competition had to be staged in isolation because it wasn't practical to vaccinate the hundreds of people who would come to watch. Earlier, a measles epidemic at Siena College near Albany had forced the school's basketball teams to play its opponents in empty gyms. Only people vaccinated before 1957 could attend. Siena had played for its conference championship in men's basketball in the Hartford Civic Center — without spectators.

Now measles had caused a similar problem for that section's 155-pounder and 250-pounder. Their matches took place in a room at a high school not far from the Onondaga County War Memorial, with only their opponents, the two referees, the coaches, a timekeeper and a few other people present. The 155-pounder, Chad MacNaughton of Glens Falls High School, was in my bracket. At first the state officials weren't going to let me wrestle because my measles shots weren't up-to-date and it was too late to get vaccinated. My father got Ron Pelligra, his 1976 national champion at heavyweight who was now an attorney in Syracuse, to prepare for a court hearing. But it didn't come to that.

MacNaughton and I both won our quarterfinal bouts and, on Saturday morning, squared off in the semifinals with only a scorer, timer, coaches and tournament representative.

What a strange experience. He and I rode to the high school in the kind of van that police use to transport criminals from jail to court. We sat toe-to-toe, neither of us knowing what to say. I had Coach Riggs and my father with me; Dad had sneaked in as the section's team trainer. MacNaughton had his coach. We wrestled, and I won, and I went into a storage closet and yelled with joy. I was a state finalist at last.

Then we had to ride back to the War Memorial in that same police van, toe-to-toe. I hid my face under a towel so he couldn't see me grinning.

At the War Memorial, the rest of my family asked what had happened. The score hadn't been announced yet. I hung my head, and allowed them to assume I'd lost and react with sympathy. Then I said, "I won."

Coach Riggs says he was numb to be coaching a wrestler in the state finals. For so many years, he'd been guiding wrestlers up in the North Country, running practices, strategizing, trying to encourage them in school and in their lives, bringing kids to the state tournament and seeing them try to get to that next level. He just couldn't believe it when I lined up with the other state finalists that Saturday night in March 1992, shook hands with Kraft, and prepared for battle.

I've heard it said that Kraft and I staged a classic match. He exploited my weakness. He took me down and let me up. In the third period I got on top and almost turned him but instead lost, 13–6.

Kraft was voted Most Outstanding Wrestler. As for me, I was disappointed, but I was kind of happy just to be in the state final. That's a natural reaction, I suppose. I still had another year to reach my goal.

That summer I went to the Olympic Training Center for a week, then off to train for a week with our Tour du Monde team. We were to represent the United States while competing in the Czech Republic and Germany. That's where I met Jason Robison, who later was a national runner-up for Edinboro University. We kept in touch, and when we were in

High school championship match against Jason Kraft

college he would come to Ohio State to train for the NCAA championships.

After the trip overseas, I went to the New York State Junior National training camp. Our 10-day camp was pretty grueling. From there, we left as a team to compete in the Junior National Championships in Minnesota. I wrestled well and went 5–2, one match away from All-American status, but I saw that I had to work on my freestyle technique. Those two months of training were exactly what I needed to prepare me for my last high school season.

Failing —
And Putting It Behind Me

(Mitch)

From the time I lost to Jason Kraft, I could hardly wait for another crack at a state title.

The state tournament was a year away, and throughout those months I thought about getting back to the championship bout and claiming my goal.

It was a long year, in that sense. My parents and I discussed whether I'd be better off in prep school. So many people send their kids to that more intense level of academic and athletic competition, either as juniors or seniors or post-grads, that it isn't too unusual. Where I grew up, hockey mattered so much that many promising players departed for prep school early, hoping it would be their ticket to a college scholarship. But I wanted my goal of a state title for my section too badly. I was comfortable in my high school, especially because Canton is one of those schools where the faculty try hard to create a positive academic experience. Even the teachers who don't care much about sports will respect and help you if you're respectful of them and try to do your work. I doubt many schools would let students call teachers by nicknames, but Canton let me call one of my teachers "Smil" because the respect was still there. I was fortunate. A prep school might've been too dog-eat-dog for me in the classroom. At least, some of my teachers thought so.

Wrestling was an afterthought in our school, compared to hockey, soccer and lacrosse, which often reached the state playoffs. Our Golden Bears hockey team ended up winning state championships four out of six years, starting when I was there. But even people in the school who didn't care much about wrestling respected me for pursuing a goal with such passion.

That state final waited for me, if all went well, but it lay months away. I went on with life. I ended up being chosen for first-team all-league and All-North in soccer, at center-midfield. That was nice, but soccer was just a way to have fun for me. I had lots of friends, and dated, but I chose to stay home on the nights when everyone else partied. I had access to a car, so it wasn't that. I just settled into a sort of narrow way of living. I wanted my goal.

On weekends, when my friends were out running around, I often played Scrabble with my mother. Scrabble is a word game where you try to make as long a word as possible, as many times as you can, out of individual letters that you choose at random. I don't know why it appealed to me, since reading was never one of my favorite things. I guess it became an outlet for my competitive nature.

I still play Scrabble as often as I can, usually against Russ Hellickson, who wants to win as badly as I do and has, somehow, managed to memorize most of the words in the Scrabble book. We play at his dining room table, two grim-faced men bending over a board. Anyone who plays with us risks getting trounced.

Sometimes I picture Russ and me squaring off in the national Scrabble tournament. At one time both Russ and I were members of the National Scrabble Association. Don't laugh. Winning the national tournament in Scrabble can get you $100,000.

Every athlete needs a confidant in school, whether it's a teacher or a secretary who has been there for years. So many things are going on within you and around you when you're in high school, whether it's school pressures or doubts about yourself or new experiences you need to absorb, so many feelings. You think about things that you won't admit to anyone except your best friends or your girlfriend — or an older person who likes and listens to kids.

Jerry Smilgin and Rick Cassara were two such people for me.

Jerry is the "Smil" I mentioned earlier. He taught social studies, had taught it since 1968. I took social studies from him as a sophomore and junior, then a government elective as a senior. He also knew sports; he'd coached varsity girls' softball for years, and junior varsity boys' soccer, and he'd officiated basketball. Rick owns a popular tavern in Canton, the Tick Tock, where the walls are covered with St. Lawrence students' caricatures and with a mural of St. Lawrence student life in the 1950s. Rick coached men's basketball at SLU in the 1960s and early 1970s, and he knows Canton and its sports.

First, Smil.

I met him in ninth grade, when he cornered me after I'd wised off to a female teacher. She told him about it. "You'll be in this building for four years. Don't piss off the wrong people," he growled at me. Smil is a big man, an ex-Marine with a powerful grip and a manner that can be stern or jovial. I wasn't seeing the jovial Smil this time. He made me apologize to the teacher. I ended up becoming friends with him. For three years I sat at a desk right against his desk at the front of the room, at his desk's center. My buddy Dave McLean sat to one side of me, in the same row.

Smil had been teaching in the same first-floor room for 13 years when I came along, and it was his private kingdom. A hundred books, at least, stood in rows around his blackboard. Most of them were about history, but some were novels. His mementoes included a shrunken head ("The last student who failed my final," he'd tell kids), a small model of a black bull (a gift from softball players who said they'd play like bulls that spring), and signs like one that read, "God made only so many perfect heads. The rest He covered with hair." Smil is bald as an egg.

I took refuge in that room many times. Along with the people who cheered me on, there were people who secretly hoped I'd fail. Maybe my personality rubbed them the wrong way, or maybe it's just another side of human nature. When someone fails, people feel relieved, as if that person were now more mortal or human. They can feel that their own failure, or their lack of trying, is OK. Smil understood this, and he understood the pressures I was under as a sectional champion who wasn't content with that achievement. My senior year, when I was a state runner-up who wanted to be more, he knew all about my feelings. Smil always appreciated wrestling even though he didn't know much about it. He liked the sportsmanship involved with the sport: the way we shook hands before and after a match, the way wrestlers maul each other and then oftentimes embrace out of respect. He would always feel badly for me when I would mope into his room, face gaunt from cutting weight. One time he asked me, "When was your last square meal?" I didn't have an answer for him.

Smil introduced me to some good books. He'd been in the Marines during the Vietnam War, and he had plenty of books about that topic. He gave me Louis L'Amour's *Last of the Breed,* about a military pilot of Native American descent who gets shot down and captured in Siberia, and escapes, surviving in the wilderness. I loved it. And when I was struggling with cutting weight one time, he told me about a Marine hero named Chesty Puller. Puller had lost both legs and had his hands mangled in Vietnam, but he persevered, trying to live normally. He wrote about it in a 1991 memoir, *Fortunate Son.*

"I think I just reinforced what your family taught you," Smil says now of my friendship with him. "Your success came from two things: family and religion. You're one of the most religious people I've ever known." He says that all of the kids in my family were always prepared, always had our homework done when we came to class. I know I tried hard in his classes. Now, several years later, I can relate to him more as a man. I always stop by his house in the summer for a beer or two. That started when I was in college. Once, early in my Ohio State days, Smil and Coach Riggs and I were having a beer at his house. They said if I ever made it to the NCAA finals, they'd be there. They were as good as their word.

Rick Cassara had been around sports and coaching a long time. He knew what the life of an athlete was like, and he warned me to take care of schoolwork as well as wrestling. He wanted me to have an existence after my athletic career was over. "You may be a great athlete, but they'll judge you as a person, not by sports," he'd tell me. I initially thought he would quit impressing that upon me once I won a national title, thinking that once I was successful as an athlete that would be enough in his eyes. But he didn't. Now, years later I realize that he was giving me the great advice.

When I won the high school national championship as a senior, he threw a big party at his restaurant for anyone who wanted to come and congratulate me. Sharing that moment with other supporters in the community made me proud to be from a small town.

By my senior season, I'd reached 6-foot-3 and had gone up to the 167 pound weight class.

I didn't give up a takedown or a point all season, until the state tournament. That was how much I'd outgrown the North Country, not to belittle my home region.

My coaches and I knew about Sirrell Gisendanner long before I met him in the state final. He was a dominant force in the Rochester area, which lies about four hours southwest of Canton, in the western part of the state. Friends in that area sent articles about Gisendanner, and we tried to get scouting reports. We knew he was enormously powerful, a weightlifter who competed on the national level. Some "wrestling people" thought I should move up a weight class to avoid Gisendanner. But my father wouldn't have any part of it. "Never dodge opponents," were his words.

The 1993 state tournament was in a building next to the Onondaga County War Memorial that year, a brand-new convention center called the Oncenter. The War Memorial was closed for renovation and asbestos removal. The state chairman for wrestling had held the tournament in Syracuse since 1971, and he didn't want to move it to another city for that year and risk losing it if people liked the new site. So he set up the

Competing in the New York high school championships

Oncenter, bringing in bleachers and setting up rows of folding chairs around the mats. It was cramped, not the best situation, and people were turned away. I was disappointed not to be competing at the War Memorial. Months before the tournament, a friend had gone to the War Memorial and grabbed a brick from the construction site. He wrote my name on it, followed by "1993 New York State Champion." I kept it on my desk until I left for the state meet.

I tried hard to focus on my life's goal: a state title.

Every year the program for the state tournament had a feature article about one of the seniors who was a favorite in his weight class. In 1993, I was the subject of that article. The writer mentioned my wish to be the first state champion from my section, and the crowd cheered me on throughout the weekend. They all appreciated the dream of a small-town boy, even the ones from Long Island, which is so different from St. Lawrence County that it seems like another country.

Gisendanner was like a big wedge of muscle, and when we squared off for the title, he capitalized on my major weakness: my struggle to control my long body and my lack of takedown ability.

My father sat by the side of the mat with his camera, yelling instructions to me. Coach Riggs pretty much deferred to him.

Gisendanner and I went back and forth. He wasn't in the best of shape, and there were times when it slowed him. I held that edge, thanks to my running in the early morning and all my other ways of training. But he was stronger and he finally went ahead, and I felt my dream slipping away.

I tied the match, 10–10, and sent it into overtime with four seconds left, scoring a takedown with an arm spin. Coach Riggs remembers that I said to him, "What can I do?" and he didn't know. Then I said, "I've got it," and went back out there and scored with the arm spin. It's part of what I call the ability to scramble, a weapon I've used throughout my career.

The crowd roared when I got my takedown, and people were so excited they leaned too much on the barriers around the mat, falling through.

I had to hold Gisendanner down just to get into overtime. It was a chore, he was so strong.

About 40 seconds into sudden-death overtime, he took me down to win, 12–10.

I just lay there motionless, staring up at the lights. I can still see them. Then I ran out of the building, to some hallway. I was so crushed, I couldn't even cry. Not until later. I finally just found my way back.

I told the press that I hoped if I couldn't be a state champion, that maybe my brother Johnny, then a sixth grader, would succeed in achieving my dream.

Gisendanner was voted Most Outstanding Wrestler, the second time that the man who defeated me in the final was chosen MOW. Again, the better man had won my dream match.

The next night I just sat home all day, crying, crushed. I was sure that everybody in Canton thought I was a failure. I doubted they'd understand what had happened.

Then, on Monday I said I was going to quit feeling sorry for myself. I needed to prepare for a new challenge, the national tournament.

Sometimes Joy Comes Unexpectedly

(Scott)

Mitch's dream was gone, vanished in a few seconds into the yellow-lit air of the Oncenter.

Sirrell Gisendanner had emerged as the better man, and there was nothing Mitch could do about it. Wrestling is like that. So is life. You deal with the joys and the pains, for each carries its own impact on your person, and you try to move on. It's easy for me to say that, of course. Sometimes you never quite leave something behind, or you think you have and then it surfaces again, years later. That happens to me because I have a phenomenal memory and I'm a writer, so I think about things more than most people. I pore over experiences years after they've occurred. Mitch? He'll remember his defeats but he'll hopefully just absorb them. Sports teaches you that.

Mitch's mother recalls finding him once, after he'd lost in the state final the second time, sitting at the dining room table with his head down.

"Mom, that was my dream," he said.

"There'll be other dreams," she said.

"I don't want any other dream."

The national high school tournament in Pittsburgh falls two weeks after the New York State tournament. When Mitch was in high school, seniors who placed in the top two in their state qualified (it's now seniors who place in the top four). As the runner-up at 167, Mitch had qualified.

He expected nothing but another experience in his career.

The week before the national championships, while practicing with the Montreal freestyle club, he tore cartilage around his sternum. Despite the pain, he decided to go to the national tournament. His father went with him. John Clark wasn't optimistic; he told Donna Clark that it wasn't worth her while to go, since Mitch might not win a match. I have a hard time picturing this, because anytime I've seen a Clark wrestle, the action is accompanied by choruses of cheers and screams of joy from his family in some corner of the arena.

As they drove down their long driveway for the trip to Pittsburgh, Mitch started to complain about his chest injury. John stopped the car and said that he wasn't in the frame of mind to drive 10 hours just to see Mitch throw in the towel in the first round as an injury default.

"What's it gonna be, Mitch, wrestle all-out with the injury or not bother with the tournament?" John asked.

"Wrestle," was Mitch's answer. He was quiet for most of the drive.

And Mitch wrestled his way to the 1993 scholastic national championship at 171.

Sometimes wonderful things happen when you least expect them.

I can think of some examples from my own life. There was the time I was elected as my homeroom representative to Student Council in 11th grade, when I thought I had no chance. We didn't campaign or speak, we just looked around the room and voted. On the first day of school I looked at who else was in my homeroom, and my heart sank. Yet I tied and then won. That happened in the fall of 1971 but I remember it as if it were last month. And there was the time two college coaches told me I'd been elected to the New York State Intercollegiate Wrestling Hall of Fame. I thought they were joking. They weren't. There was a new category for contributors. I'd photographed and written about wrestling so much over the years, both in my job as a sports writer for the Syracuse newspapers and in my spare time, that the coaches had decided to give me this honor. It completely humbled me.

Mitch felt no pressure for the national tournament. He was totally relaxed, giving him the ability to completely open up his strategy. He was about to be surprised.

Wess Audsley, the former St. Lawrence heavyweight who had be-friended Mitch and encouraged him to come to summer camp at Ohio State, joined John Clark in Mitch's corner. "I didn't think it would last too long. I thought he would be eliminated at the beginning," Wess says now. "It ended up being one of the most enjoyable experiences of my life. Here was Mitch, going against guys who were state champions — and not just state champions once but several times, in some cases. And he kept winning."

Celebrating quarterfinals win over Aaron Simpson in high school nationals

Mitch had hoped for another crack at Gisendanner, but the New York champion wasn't there. The field was still loaded; six of the wrestlers at 171, including Mitch, were later Division I All-Americans. They included two NCAA runners-up, Jason Robison of Edinboro at 190 and Brandon Slay of UPenn at 167, plus two time All-American Aaron Simpson.

Mitch faced Aaron Simpson, four-time Arizona state champ, in the quarterfinals — and pinned him. He pinned four of his last five opponents.

"John and I kept laughing and hitting each other on the shoulder," Wess says. "Mitch would beat some three-time Iowa champ, and we'd say, 'Well, we won't see that again.' Then he'd beat the next guy. In the final, he had this kid from Maryland who was so good, he was on the ASICS poster for high school wrestling. And Mitch pinned this guy too."

Mitch's opponent in the final was four-time Maryland champion Grant Johnson. Mitch fell behind, 4–1. When it was his choice to take the top or bottom position, he decided to take the top position. Johnson made what John Clark considered a mistake; he tried a granby roll while Mitch had a half nelson ride going. "Mitch knew how to stop it," John says.

Mitch pinned Johnson.

When the referee slapped the mat, Mitch ran into the open arms of his father and Wess Audsley. His father yelled in one ear that he loved Mitch, while Audsley yelled into the other ear that Mitch had just won himself $60,000, meaning a full scholarship. Mitch says he was so elated "because I had never won a major tournament. It was such a surprising and exciting moment."

Mitch never chose bottom very often from then on. His "take top" philosophy was born.

He was chosen "Most Outstanding Wrestler."

"So amazing," says Wess Audsley. "Like finding gold in a garbage can."

Mitch had been recruited by Ohio State, Lock Haven, Syracuse, Wisconsin and North Carolina. At Ohio State, Russ Hellickson had recruited him mostly at Audsley's urging, and because the Clarks were old friends. Hellickson hadn't offered much scholarship aid. But now Mitch was a national champion. College coaches swarmed to him that weekend, asking him to visit. Hellickson's interest grew immediately. Audsley's argument was that the only guy Mitch had to work out with over the years was his father, on the living room carpet.

"I can't spend a lot of time recruiting outside Ohio, our state is so rich in wrestling," he says. "If I'm going to go outside Ohio to recruit, I have

Maryland's Grant Johnson controls Mitch moments before Mitch scores a fall in the 1993 national high school final

to be convinced it's worth it. Sure, I knew Mitch's family, but his winning the national title convinced me."

Wess Audsley saw a remarkable thing after Mitch won: he showed his humility and loyalty.

*Mitch and Dad with MOW trophy,
1993 high school nationals in Pittsburg*

John Clark wanted Mitch to go home to a hero's welcome. But Mitch had promised his friends from Canton that he would go with them on spring break in Florida. As Audsley remembers it, Mitch told all of his new friends in the coaching ranks that he would talk to them after he got back from Florida. "Instead of assuming the mantle of stud wrestler, Mitch reverted to being Mitch," Audsley says. "He showed his true colors. He told everybody, 'I'm getting on a bus and sitting for 20 hours, to go on spring break.' "

"Dad said, 'Come home, there are a lot of people who want to speak to you, you can take the car to Florida later,' " Mitch remembers. "I asked, 'Where was that offer last week when I bought Greyhound tickets to and from Florida?' "

Mitch got his hero's reception in Canton later. His high school hung a huge portrait of him with his national MOW trophy on the gymnasium wall, where it still hangs. The only other athlete up there was basketball player Hal Cohen, Class of 1976, who had once sunk 598 consecutive free throws one day after school and who had gone on to play for Syracuse University.

That spring was a great time for Mitch. He took all of his recruiting trips and let himself be wined and dined. Canton set aside a Mitch Clark Day, and Rick Cassara held a party at his restaurant that was open to the public. Mitch had time to start dating again and enjoying moments like the Senior Prom, where he was voted Prom King, followed by graduation.

Still, he was not a state champion. That knowledge lurked in his mind and fueled his desire even years later.

Mitch didn't say this to many people, but he told his mother that he'd trade the national title for a state title. That, after all, had been his dream.

He signed a letter of intent with Ohio State.

He never faced Sirrell Gisendanner or Grant Johnson again.

Freshman   in   the   Big   Ten

(Mitch)

Sometimes dreaming hurts. If you don't accomplish what you dreamed of, you may shy away from dreaming again. Don't.

I headed off to college with a need for new dreams. The old ones were gone.

I accepted the scholarship to Ohio State partly because I'd known Russ Hellickson all my life and partly because of Wess Audsley. Columbus, Ohio, is a nice city with lots to do. I trusted Russ with my future as a wrestler. Not to mention the fact that the Big Ten is the best conference in our sport, maybe any sport.

There's nothing quite like the first few months of college. You have to find your way around campus — a huge campus of 55,000 students, in OSU's case — and figure out what classes to take. You have so much freedom, no parents to tell you when to study and go to bed. I've heard it said so many times, but you can't know what it's like until you're there, a young adult on your own, meeting people, in my case living in a different part of the nation.

I saw one familiar face: Rob Archer, a freshman from West Virginia. We'd met in tenth grade, when I went to a Junior National training camp in West Virginia. I didn't know this then, but he'd thought I was so obnoxious when we met at the training camp, he was glad to see me leave. Then, when we were high school seniors, I ran into him at the national tournament. Apparently I told him that one of his opponents, a kid from New York, was real tough — and good luck. "Thanks a lot," he said to himself then — he didn't need to hear that. Then, later that year, Rob was looking at a *U.S.A. Wrestling* magazine issue that lists where all the best seniors across the nation are going to college. He saw that only two were going to Ohio State: himself and me. His friends needled him about it. But in time we became friends, and by the time we finished our careers five years later, we were as tight as two buddies can be. He was my housemate and soulmate. We laughed often about those earlier times when we'd met.

The Big Ten added an intensity to it all. It's such a powerful conference in college sports, not just football, and from the beginning you know that athletics is going to run your life at times. The whole thing feels like a business, like you have a job to do — not just the job your high school coach always told the team it had to get done, a *real* job. You know this when you arrive, and you savor the idea that you're among the best. You try to rise to the challenge of being on a team where everyone was among the best, not just in his league but in his state. Maybe the idea intimidates you, but you have to shake it off.

Walk through the football complex at Ohio State and see the indoor practice field, the weight room where former Buckeyes now in the National Football League work out with the current players in the off-season, the massive locker rooms, the display cases with Eddie George's Heisman Trophy and a cluster of other mementoes. Go to a football game at Ohio Stadium and see 89,800 people who live for those autumn weekends. Go to lunch as a high school senior, during your recruiting trip, at the Buckeye Cafe and Hall of Fame, where the halls are lined with display cases full of football jerseys, pictures of Woody Hayes, and basketballs with names like John Havlicek on them. See the pictures of golfer Jack Nicklaus and track immortal Jesse Owens. Get a Big Ten champion in any sport to show you his or her championship ring, a magnificent testament to achievement. Feel the respect granted those athletes who excel.

This is the Big Ten. This is where I set new goals.

As a freshman, I had no goal other than survival at first. I didn't aim to break into the Buckeyes' lineup right away. They had Kevin Randleman at 177 pounds, a two-time national champion, a stud.

Then Kevin decided not to wrestle his senior year, and I stepped into his spot for the 1993–94 season. I began to learn from Russ and from Rex Holman, one of our assistant coaches who'd gone undefeated and won the national championship at 190 the previous year.

I went 15–5, with nine pins.

I had the fastest pin of the season: 44 seconds, over Troy Jindra of Simon Fraser University at the Oregon Wrestling Classic.

Mitch chooses top against Weldon in the 1997 NCAA final

The Clark family pictured in March 1989 issue of Good Housekeeping Magazine
Left to right: Charlie, Mary, Johnny, Sarah, Mitch, Nicki and Christy

Big Ten action, Mitch vs. longtime rival Jevon Hermon of Illinois

*Mitch turning Vertus Jones of West Virginia during the
1998 NCAA Championship bout*

*Brother Johnny becomes New York State High School Champion
two weeks before Mitch becomes National Champion*

*ESPN commentator and Olympic Gold Medallist Jeff Blatnick interviews
Mitch after the 1998 NCAA Championship*

Then disaster struck. I failed a math course and got a 1.75 grade point average for the fall quarter. You need a 1.8 to compete in sports as a freshman, a 2.0 after that.

I was academically ineligible. So was Rob Archer. "Two 18-year-olds who didn't know anything," is how he sums it up now.

So embarrassing. I remember Russ's talking to me about it. He said, "You guys need to go figure out what to do." It was the worst week of my life. I tried to talk to my professors, to see if I could do something about my grades, but none of them budged. The university tested me to see if I was learning-disabled. I'd always struggled in school, which was probably one reason I disliked it. This was another reason my parents thought about sending me to prep school, for academics as well as wrestling. The tests showed I was close, but not quite learning-disabled. I would've been eligible if I'd turned out to need help.

I was crushed. I felt I'd let down Wess Audsley, my team, my family. My parents changed a little at that point, didn't treat me with that same respect. I became eligible again 10 weeks later, but by then the season was over.

I think part of it was the strain of adjusting to being a college athlete in Division I. My body wasn't used to the training and travel schedule. At Ohio State we practiced and either worked out with weights or ran in a separate session every day. I would also wake up for two months straight, so sore I could barely move. And I wasn't getting along with my roommate, an urban kid who was my opposite. Because of my situation, after that year Russ tried to arrange it so wrestlers were roommates with other wrestlers. Many universities do that. It makes sense anyway, since you'll both be on roughly the same schedule.

Rob used to tell me that we'd be OK, we'd study and get back to the wrestling program. I was down, and I'd say it didn't matter, I'd transfer somewhere. I didn't transfer, of course. College athletes often think about transferring when times are tough, but usually it's just a passing thought. I remained with the Buckeyes.

Before I lost my spot in the lineup, I was getting to know my teammates. That's a key part of being a freshman, the new guy, the rookie.

Eric Smith was the 158-pounder that season, a sophomore. Eric is black, and he hung out with the other black guys on the team, including

Dunyasha Yetts, the senior 142-pounder who would end up being an All-American. It was no big deal, they just hung out together, and roomed together.

"We were on that road trip to Oregon," Eric says, "and you came into our room, this room that had three black guys in it. You just had your boxer shorts on. You came in, climbed into one of the beds, and said, 'Let's talk.' It was pretty gutsy for a freshman."

Veterans hung out with other veterans who were good at wrestling. They didn't really hang out with new guys.

"We all were laughing," Eric says. "You can be friends with anybody."

Eventually I figured out how to juggle school and wrestling. Universities have all sorts of support services for student athletes, to help you with that. Beyond those services, you just basically find that the busier you are, the more you get done. You get into a schedule and become productive. I made lists of my top 10 things to get done. Every student athlete lives with the stress of keeping his or her life balanced. If you're doing well at your sport, ironically, your schoolwork might be hurting. You can't let things overwhelm you or try to tackle life as a whole. You must go piece by piece. When you're at practice, focus on practice. Choose a major well, choose one you like, one that will be rewarding. What you major in is not as important as what you get out of college.

Chapter Ten

The Well-Rounded Athlete

(Mitch)

Anyone who has gone to high school or college, or paid attention to what's covered in the news media, knows that being an athlete in America is special. It's been that way for decades. People who excel at games matter. They're respected, admired, even worshipped. Their opinions matter more than they sometimes should. Athletes are also despised by some people who don't have the physical ability or the will power or dedication to play a sport. These people automatically think that athletes are stupid or want special treatment from fellow students, teachers and other adults.

As an athlete, I was the center of attention in school even when I didn't want to be. It grew more intense when I became a state placewinner, then more intense again when I was state runner-up. I'm pretty outgoing, pretty vocal, and I'm tall, so I always stood out.

I've talked so far about some facets of being an athlete. Now I want to focus on a few other topics about an athlete's life in high school and college.

The News Media

I've been talking to newspaper writers and television reporters since sometime in junior high. Canton sits in a rural region with little press. My school was covered by a weekly newspaper in Canton that belonged to a chain, meaning some stories might appear in the daily newspaper 20 miles away in Ogdensburg that covered the whole league. A daily newspaper in Watertown, 65 miles away, covered our league using two sports writers based at its Canton bureau. The Watertown television station did some pieces on high school sports in my league. I'm sure plenty of high school athletes out there face much more media attention, especially football and basketball players in more metropolitan areas, or in small towns where people never hear enough about sports, but I thought I received plenty of media attention. Even if it's just one little article, you still had to learn how to talk to people with notebooks and microphones, you still had to answer questions clearly, your neighbors and the other kids in school still read it. It intrigues me to see how some student athletes sign their letter of intent in front of a slew of media reporters. It's different in the North Country — not as big a deal. I honestly don't even remember signing the papers.

I wasn't good at live interviews on electronic media when I was in high school, but I learned. You should say what's on your mind, try to avoid being redundant, try to tell them something unique. Try to avoid cliches — you know, those phrases people say over and over that sound so trite. It's tough because coaches might encourage you to stick with cliches like "I just want to win for the team." You may be sincere in believing the words behind those worn-out expressions, but try to put new life into what you say.

Teammates may be jealous of you for being the subject of newspaper articles. Be modest about it. Take the attention in stride.

Dealing with the news media is about people relations. It's about trying to get a clear idea of what you want to convey about yourself, about knowing writers and electronic media people as well as you can so you can communicate effectively, and about deciding when to trust a media person. It's easy to get so friendly with a member of the news media that you say too much or say something inappropriate.

You have to get used to seeing your comments in print. If you don't like the way it came out, keep that in mind the next time you talk to the news media.

I always treated every reporter the same, no matter how small the publication or listener base (in radio). I consider myself an ambassador for my sport. Let people see that wrestlers are intelligent, good people.

You may think some of a writer's questions are dumb. Be patient, be adaptable. Don't laugh at the question. Try to redirect it into something important or better suited to the occasion.

I always assume that the journalist doesn't know much about wrestling. You must be understanding and work with them. Volunteer information, expand on what you're feeling, go beyond the question.

Media people will listen to you but don't be surprised if they're thinking about the next question. Don't get upset about it.

Remember, too, how fickle the press can be. I actually got more media attention as a high school wrestler in Canton than when I competed for Ohio State. High school wrestling is huge in Ohio but it isn't covered much. Though the *Columbus Dispatch* and the daily student paper wrote about Buckeye wrestling, and interviewed me, they didn't write much when I became a national champion as a senior.

Being involved with the opposite sex

When you're an athlete in training it's always hard to have a girlfriend, no matter how much you warn her about the little time you have together, because you're tired or busy. She'll never understand. So I always shied away from having a steady girlfriend. I've often seen my teammates struggle with this. On the other hand some wrestlers have managed to have a girlfriend during the season because it's been a meaningful distraction.

Having a girlfriend can be healthy — during wrestling season it can be a needed distraction.

A month to two months before a major tournament, such as the Big Ten or nationals in my case, don't even think about starting a new relationship. A new relationship is hard work and very time consuming.

Student life

I believe there are some points in the season when you must put wrestling first — above friends and social life, even above schoolwork. It's not long, a couple of weeks maybe, but you have to do it.

As a college student, you won't have the life that people think you have. I know a lot of people because I'm outgoing. I don't hate anybody, least of all my opponents. That's something Russ Hellickson believes in; he's like that with the Russian who beat him for the Olympic gold medal. But as a student I had my priorities. Many times I'd be working out or traveling with the team while other students were partying, hanging out, doing what most students do. I used to tell my parents that my social life on weekends during the season consisted of calling them to tell how I did in a match. I wasn't joking.

Respect for your sport

Wrestling isn't pretty. It's about raw force mixed with timing and cunning. It's about pain, and sweating buckets during a match, and finding yourself in some situations that look odd to outsiders.

So let's assume that you hear people in school or in your town mutter about what a barbaric sport it is, or how crude it is. Maybe the real ignorant ones say that it's hard to watch two half-naked guys wrapped around each other.

I used to really wish I had these people for one practice, so they could see how hard you push your body. Anyone who's ever wrestled around, just with friends or whoever on the living room carpet, knows that one minute into it they're real tired. But that's just a mild taste of what we go through.

Anytime kids said to me that wrestling was sexual, I'd say, "Listen, let's have a one-on-one, just you and me." It wasn't the smartest way but it worked. There's nothing sexual about it.

It's frustrating when people belittle your sport without knowing what's going on. You work so hard, and then you have to hear that.

Most people in the U.S. think wrestling is the World Wrestling Federation. They think it's the amateur version of that stuff on TV. If one more person asks me if I'm going to the WWF next, I swear I'll lose it.

It's up to us wrestlers to make the sport more suitable for fans to watch. We need to be offensive, to wrestle with a lot of heart and intensity. If we turn it into a defensive battle, even I wouldn't want to watch it. Too many wrestlers are playing the out-of-bounds line, scooting out, calling for timeouts. Think of a match as a way to showcase your training and talents. STAND OUT. STAND ALONE. MAKE IT HAPPEN!

Learning, Redshirting — and Life in the Practice Room

(Mitch)

I came back to the Ohio State lineup as a sophomore in 1994–95 and fashioned a good record, 27–16, with 12 pins — first on the team. I placed seventh in the Big Ten tournament. That season was a natural progression in my career, not just in terms of wins and losses, but in terms of my learning what wrestling at that level was all about. I had some good teachers.

The guys who surround you, who are there in the practice room all the time and with you on road trips, are just as important as anyone else.

At Ohio State our practice room is an athletic complex that also houses intramurals and recreation. Our locker room is off the main locker room that students, faculty and staff use. The practice room is just above us, up either a staircase or a spiral staircase. It's a good-sized room lined with pictures of our All-Americans and lists of the team captains over the years. It's got big windows on one end. On the other end, where we come in, it's got workout machines and, on a wall, a round black NCAA emblem. We slap that NCAA emblem when we walk in and when we leave to remind ourselves why we are there.

Team captains are named after the season. Russ does it that way because he got tired of guys being elected captain and then not making the lineup, or not performing the way he thought a captain should. You never know who it's going to be. I was chosen twice.

I had workout partners who pushed me. Anyone who wrestles knows how important that is.

At that point the guys who pushed me were Rick Monge, Eric Smith, Mike Schyk and Rex Holman. Mike and Rex had graduated in 1993 and were there as assistant coaches. Rick was a senior in 1994–95 and Eric was a junior. Those guys just had a lot of pride, wouldn't give up anything to me, and I had to fight for my points against them. I learned how to scramble, a trait that became one of my trademarks. Those guys would beat up on me, and I'd never give up. We'd make each other work for every takedown.

They'd shoot in, and at the last second I'd readjust my hips to prevent them from taking me down. Most people, if they know they're being taken down, will just stop. I'd go head-to-head with those guys. I didn't want to give up a point, and if I did, I wanted to make sure I'd get up and score the next point.

You must find the best guys in the room who will push you and get you in shape. There were days, as a freshman, when I'd get mauled. For six weeks in a row I'd get beaten up and be sore. That's what it was about.

If you're having a bad day in practice (and everyone has them), devote a day to getting as tired as you can. Don't just shut down and quit and feel sorry for yourself. As a coach, there's nothing better to watch than two guys going at it like there's everything on the line.

Some people think they can just go into a match and wrestle hard, even if they haven't trained hard during the week. It's almost impossible. Your performance in competition is directly related to what you did in the wrestling room. If you've done the job, you'll have more confidence.

It so happens I performed better in competition than in practice. I'm glad it worked out that way, instead of the reverse. But I tried to work hard. In high school I had a poster that quoted Jim Jordan, the former two-time NCAA champion from Wisconsin: "The amount of confidence you have is directly proportional to how hard you have worked."

It isn't enough to just work hard. To be a champion, you have to understand your weaknesses and strengths, and figure out ways to compensate for weaknesses. Luck doesn't hurt. Neither does confidence.

Eric Smith ended up claiming All-American status at 158 pounds twice, placing fourth that season and fifth as a senior. But before he ever made it to that victory stand at the NCAA Championships, I knew he was a seriously competitive man. I learned that in the practice room.

He was a leader, poised, willing to speak his mind. Russ relied on him to raise his teammates to the next level of intensity with his own intensity, the way two-time national champion and three-time Big Ten champion Kevin Randleman had before I arrived, the way national champion Lee Kemp had in the late 1970s at Wisconsin, when Russ was an assistant coach there. He wanted Eric to get in our faces when we didn't perform and be there for us, urging us on.

Eric grew up in Dayton, the second of four kids. His father was a data processor at a post office. Eric's family grew to 10 kids one year, when they took in the six children of a woman who was shot to death. "My father provided for us real well, but at Christmas he might give more gifts to those kids we'd taken in," he says. "He just said they needed the gifts more."

Like me, Eric needed help to develop as a wrestler. Unlike me, he didn't get it. He learned our sport almost on his own, "by loving it," by being chosen for the national team and going to camps. Like me, he surprised people. His breakthrough came in 10th grade, when he was .500 during the season but did well in the district tournament. He placed third in the state as a senior, prompting Russ to recruit him.

Eric was one of the teammates who taught me the value of relaxing and being a clown when it was needed. The other one was Nick Nutter, our heavyweight, who was such a goof that you forgot how intense he could be. Eric says Nick "was never serious until 10 seconds before his own match. He'd be joking on the team bench two matches before his own." So Eric was the perfect blend of joker and leader, and I tried to emulate him as a junior and senior. He helped me learn about tournament wrestling too. Seeded eighth in the NCAA Championships that year, he defeated the top seed by one point and made it to the semifinals before losing, and placed fourth. "I was mad because it's all or nothing for me," he says. "I lost two matches (semifinal and third-place) by two points." His motivation: as a sophomore, he'd been ranked eighth in the Big Ten and then lost his first two matches. "It was so hard to face people after that," he says, "it drove me the last two years."

Nick Nutter taught me some of the same things that Eric did. The difference is, he was seldom serious until he had to be. It was amazing how he could switch gears.

He was the guy who, when you gave him a ride somewhere, would slap the side of the car as you were putting it in gear, making you panic that something mechanical was wrong. He was the guy who found a way to make everyone laugh.

He was also the guy who, in order to qualify for the All-American round at the 1996 NCAA tournament as a junior, needed to beat an opponent from Illinois who had already beaten him twice that season. For once, he was nervous. He and assistant coach Rex Holman went out in the arena hallway "to look at people," and Holman said that if Nick won, he'd give Nick his Doc Martin boots. Nick won, and placed seventh at heavyweight, and he still has the boots.

Nick grew up in Medina, Ohio, and came to Ohio State as a 177-pounder, growing to 190 and then, the last two seasons, heavyweight. Like me, and like our teammate Rob Archer, he was coached by his father. Like us, he found that difficult at times. Nick once said, "My dad dragged me to a match when I was four. I'd much rather be a good golfer than a good wrestler."

After he graduated in 1997, he stayed in Columbus and tried Ultimate Fighting, recruited by Mark Coleman, Ohio State's 1988 NCAA champ at 190, who had been making a living at it. He was there when I won the title in 1998. I still talk to him whenever I can. He's still the master at making us all laugh.

I decided to redshirt in 1995–96. That means training with the team but not competing. My weight class was very strong, with Les Gutches of Oregon State at the top.

A lot of guys on my team were upset with me, and that was tough, because I was so close to them. They knew we'd have a good team, a better one with me. We ended up having three All-Americans that year: Eric, Nick and Charlie Beck, who was second at 150. My teammates thought we could have been top ten nationally — we placed 14th.

But I made a good decision. When you redshirt, you can practice with the team and not much else. So I was with the team but not truly part of it, and I used the time to look at what I needed to improve on. The team concept is important, but you must look out for yourself. Then, in the long run, you'll help the team even more.

I competed in off-season and open tournaments. I got stronger. I was small for 177, just 180 in the off-season, and I gained 20 pounds that year.

It was hard to see my team lose when it might've won if I'd been in the lineup. And the team told me that a few times. But, as my mom reminded me, things work out. Which turned out to be true.

Chapter Twelve

Like a Second Father

(Scott)

I first knew Russ Hellickson as a figure on a poster, then as a big, bearish man who filled St. Lawrence's summer wrestling camp with his booming mix of geniality and intensity. He was an Olympic silver medalist, a sports god, who carried himself as a regular guy. That poster, which showed him about to throw his Iranian opponent in the bout for the 1976 Olympic gold medal at 220 pounds, graced the wall of many a young wrestler's bedroom and many a coach's office. He was one of a handful of men who shaped American wrestling in the 1970s. I don't remember meeting him at the camp, but I remember the excitement that preceded his annual week of teaching. Later, when I was writing and editing a newspaper about wrestling in New York with Mitch Clark's father, Russ was publishing a similar newspaper in his native Wisconsin.

The next time I saw Russ was in January 1999 at Ohio State's practice room, where he paced the sides of the mats, studying the Buckeyes and plainly wishing he could mix it up with them. He'd by then given up wrestling with his team everyday because his body ached from old injuries — neck, back, knees. One day he wore a suit and tie to the mid-day practice session. He'd already spoken to students at a middle school and was planning to speak to a Rotary Club that afternoon. He looked as if he wanted to throw off his suit, loosen his tie and lock up with the 197-pounders.

Russ was a 10-time freestyle national champion. He was a three-time Pan American Games champion; there is only one other, Bruce Baumgartner. He has been a television commentator for U.S. coverage of Olympic wrestling since 1984 and will be again in 2000. He captained the 1980 Olympic freestyle team, but that team did not compete because of the U.S. boycott by President Jimmy Carter of the Moscow Games.

He has been head coach at two Big Ten universities, Wisconsin and Ohio State. As a head coach, and as a Wisconsin assistant, he has coached wrestlers to All-American status 61 times and to NCAA championships 16 times. He is an inductee of the National Wrestling Hall of Fame (1989) and Wisconsin Athletic Hall of Fame (1996). He is a world traveler at home in big cities. Yet when I talk to him, I sense I'm with a plainspoken Midwestern farm boy who sees things with hard-won wisdom. He wants to win so badly, yet he thinks sports is just one part of the whole picture.

No wonder Mitch calls him "my second father."

Russ Hellickson grew up on a dairy farm near Stoughton, Wisconsin. He says his high school coach didn't know much about wrestling but was a great motivator, a skill he has tried to emulate. He played football for two years and wrestled for three at the University of Wisconsin at Madison, finishing second in the Big Ten twice. He says that at the time he graduated in 1970, wrestling was "my whole life." He thought about little besides getting better, focusing on his goals. And he became a wrestling icon.

Along the way, he married his wife Nancy and became a father of three daughters. Mitch thinks he regards his wrestlers as the sons he never had, dispensing advice on more than just sports. Certainly this is true in Mitch's case.

Russ was Wisconsin's head coach for four seasons, guiding the Badgers to second place in the Big Ten in 1985 and 1986. Then he moved to Ohio State for the 1986–87 season and has coached the Buckeyes to performances as high as third in the Big Ten (1991, 1992, 1993) and fourth in the NCAA (1991).

"My goal has always been to win the Big Ten and the NCAA, and that hasn't happened," he says, quickly noting that nobody else has emerged as champion much either, with Iowa in the conference. When Minnesota won the 1999 Big Ten tournament, it was the first time in 25 years that Iowa hadn't claimed it. The Hawkeyes have dominated the NCAA Championships, with 17 titles, including the last five.

"Every exceptional wrestler I ever had, especially the Big Ten and national champions, was unique but had one constant: they were driven to win," Russ said one day, seated in his office at Ohio Stadium. "They all believe they can win. And Mitch was the most extreme of all. You could just see it."

Over the years Mitch was this little kid hanging around the mats at St. Lawrence's camp and running around at the Clark family's summer home. Years later, at Buckeye Wrestling Camp, Russ saw a tall, skinny kid who needed to improve what he did on his feet. Russ recruited him only after he won the 1993 high school national title. He resisted any impulse to change Mitch's unorthodox style, even as he set about teaching the young man how to use his abilities to win on the college level.

"Mitch never moped after a loss," he says. "A loss was like a stimulus — 'OK, I'm not quite there, what do I have to do?' To a lot of people, a loss is a failure, but not to Mitch. I tended to take losses hard. When I lost in the Olympics, and ended up taking the silver medal, I wouldn't talk to anybody much for two weeks. Mitch was unpredictable in technique and strategy. He would do things to see if they worked. He was hard to finish on because he never stopped movin'. He has a lot of grit and heart. He'll wear you down, always keep coming."

Russ had some trying times.

Mitch was destined to be a Buckeye . . . On the Jersey shore, 1977

His brother died in a farm accident in 1975. His father died in the summer of 1998. Russ underwent open-heart surgery in 1996. He sometimes dislikes what he sees in the 1990s. When he talks about college sports, he sounds discontented, like many men from the 1960s and 1970s who have been forced to adjust to a changed landscape of gender equity battles, more rules, more paperwork and politics. He's happiest when he's recruiting a wrestler from a rural school or speaking to a group in some small town, driving the back roads.

He also savors his Scrabble battles with Mitch, who began playing with him the summer before his freshman year, beginning a special friendship. They play at Russ's kitchen table, in the comfortable house where the den is decorated with Russ's many awards and honors, including the silver medal. Like Wess Audsley, Russ has taken pleasure in getting to know Mitch as a young adult. They are much alike, both dry of humor, both personable, both rural boys who've learned to make their way in an urban land.

Russ says the toughest thing about doing commentary on television is talking while you listen to the producer's voice in your headphones. You're tempted to stop while you listen to what the producer is saying, but you can't stop.

Dan DiCesare, Mitch, Russ Hellickson, and Rob Archer

Mitch laughs about Russ's obsession with travel plans. "He gets stressed out when we're on the road," Mitch says. "It's a team joke. He'll get us to the airport three hours before a flight. Once, when I won a Big Ten title, I came off the mat and Russ congratulated me and said, 'Now, we have a plane to catch.' I said, 'Russ, I just won a Big Ten title.' He said, 'I know, but we have a plane to catch.'"

Russ, in turn, thinks Mitch will make a good coach because he'll see in his wrestlers the hunger that made Mitch a champion. It's a hunger Russ also recognizes as a coach. In that, too, they are alike.

Russ has changed as a coach in recent years. Some would say he has mellowed, not in his will to win but in his feeling for where wrestling lies in the overall picture. Watching the Buckeyes run one evening, he said that years earlier he would've been furious if anyone lagged behind the rest as the group jogged around the track. Now he sees some wrestlers running well in sprints during the workout and some excelling at the longer races, and he thinks it reflects their different abilities to explode during a match. He sees athletes more as individuals than he used to, and looks for ways to motivate them as individuals.

"If I had Mitch the first five years I was a coach, I'd have ruined him," he says. "I would've tried to change him. I've become more mellow. If you're a kid with a lot of heart, a kid who understands what he wants and will work to get it, I'm good for you." His bottom line: athletics is not that important in itself. It's "an educational tool, all about learning about yourself, what can I learn from this to make me a better person."

Not that he hates defeat any less. After the Buckeyes lost to Pittsburgh in January 1999, winning only three bouts, Russ was so upset he left the building without talking to his team. He left his assistant coaches, including Mitch, who joined the coaching staff after his eligibility ran out, to explain just how disappointed he was. Much as he likes his wrestlers, and sees them as people, he expects them to produce. That's life in the Big Ten. That's what made him an Olympic medalist.

NCAA Runner-Up

(Mitch)

After redshirting in what would have been my junior year, I was ready. I was now in my fourth year of college, coming into my own. I was getting stronger, getting better on my feet (though still a long way from where I wanted to be). All summer I'd lifted like crazy and loaded up on the supplements (Designer Protein and Creatine). It put on a lot of muscle. I like to think of my summer workouts as putting money in the bank for the long winter.

I was past being one of the rookies or guys on the bottom of the wrestling team's pecking order. Eric Smith was gone, graduated, though still around and quite willing to give me his views after matches. There was that strange feeling, when the previous year's seniors aren't in

The pressure's off, momentarily

the practice room anymore and the team has a whole new look and feel.

I started off by placing second in the Las Vegas Open, one of the tougher early-season tournaments. That was the beginning of an amazing season. I went 38–5, fourth in school history in winning percentage for a season with .884 (I surpassed it as a senior, when I was 39–1, or .975). I set a school record for team points with 165.5 (I broke that as a senior too, with 181.5). I had 16 pins.

I won the Michigan Open with a pin in the title bout over Erich Harvey of Michigan State, who was ranked No. 1 at the time. I was trailing 4–1, and I pinned him after I took top.

Then I became a Big Ten champion, beating Jevon Herman of Illinois in the finals. I was in awe of my conference, the best conference in college wrestling, and it was hard for me to put aside that awe and go out there to wrestle for the championship. I always got a lot of satisfaction out of beating any kid from the Big Ten, even if I was heavily favored. Herman was ranked ninth nationally and seeded second. I was seeded first and defeated him, 5–3.

I haven't said much about my "take top" philosophy, though I keep referring to it. The idea started in high school and intensified at the national high school tournament, where I took top and pinned Grant Johnson of Maryland in the title bout. I rarely chose bottom again.

Most people (in college) just try to ride guys and get riding time. I feel my best chances to score are when I'm on top. It's a risk, but it's worth taking. My whole thing was that on any given day, I could pin any guy in the nation.

My team point totals for my junior and senior seasons seem to justify it.

I see wrestlers in high school take top, but not too many in college. It's the easiest place to score points from, because most wrestlers don't train in ways to counter it. They train for when they're being ridden or when they're being let up so their opponent can try a takedown on them. When you crank on your opponent, he's not used to it, not used to defending against it.

My teammate Eric Odita always said he felt sorry for guys who hadn't wrestled me before.

My career was following the sort of logical incline that everyone wishes he could have. People who adapt and try to improve are the ones who succeed at the collegiate level. I had decided to master new things. I had decided to be better on my feet. In the off-season I competed in freestyle a lot more, because freestyle wrestling emphasizes takedowns.

You have to earn the national championship in wrestling. It isn't based on rankings, as it is in football.

I was living in a house near campus with a couple of teammates and a couple of friends who weren't wrestlers. The good thing about living with teammates is, you're on the same wavelength during the season. You share whatever is happening with the team. The bad thing is, if you're winning and they aren't, you have to step lightly sometimes. It keeps you humble.

By now my two closest friends on the team were Robbie Archer, the 126-pounder from West Virginia who had disliked me in high school but gotten used to me at Ohio State, and Dan DiCesare, a local boy who had walked on and become a starter at 150 and 158. They were two of my housemates.

Rob grew up five blocks from the convention center in Huntington where West Virginia holds its state tournament. His parents run the tournament. His dad, Bill, was the 1998 National Coach of the Year. After Rob graduated in 1998, he returned to his hometown to teach in a middle school and help his dad coach.

Robbie and I had been buddies since we'd shared the trauma of being academically ineligible as freshmen. We could talk to each other about any problem. We're built the same way, long and lean, and we wrestled for our fathers, and we both got stronger by pushing cars.

In the off-season he and I had something called the Seven Sets of Hell, a workout we did twice a week on the hip sled. This workout is better known as the Seven Sets O' Seven.

The routine starts with doing seven reps on the sled, then a 30-second break.

Then it unfolds like this:

> 7 reps, 15-second break
> 7 reps, 10-second break
> 7 reps, 10-second break
> 7 reps, 15-second break
> 7 reps, 30-second break

You do seven reps again, and the exercise is finished.

It took us five minutes to complete our lift. The Seven Sets of Hell was painful, especially if you put enough weight on to be doing "negatives" on each set.

We'd push each other until we cried, we were so tired, and it gave each of us a mental edge. Athletes from other teams at Ohio State used to marvel at our work ethic when they saw grown, tough men whimpering and often crying on the machine. On a couple of occasions, they told me that I inspired them to work harder or have reestablished what they thought was hard work. That is what leading through example is all about.

I had my rivalries with Jevon Herman of Illinois, and Rob Neidlinger of Penn State, and Aaron Simpson of Arizona State. Rob's biggest rival was Jason Betz of Penn State. We always liked wrestling against Penn State in State College, Pennsylvania, but Rob liked it more because it was so close to his West Virginia roots. Rob beat Betz as a junior, in the dual meet, then lost to him in the Big Ten tournament. When we were seniors, the Nittany Lions came to Columbus for our annual match, and Rob beat Betz again, on national TV.

I always wished Rob would have been able to accomplish his goals, but it wasn't to be. In my opinion, he cut so much weight that it was hard for him to improve, because 75 percent of the time he was working to keep his weight down. Rob placed eighth in the Big Ten as a junior, a respectable finish. He didn't place as a senior, though that year both of his losses at the Big Ten tournament were to All-Americans. So he didn't reach what he'd hoped to. But as a junior and as a senior, he shared the team award for Most Dedicated.

Dan DiCesare grew up in Dublin, Ohio, and went to a Catholic school in Columbus, Bishop Watterson. Cut from the basketball team in eighth grade, he turned to wrestling, then tried out for basketball again the next year. He didn't want to wrestle because it meant following a successful older brother, but the coach coaxed him into it.

Dan was a sectional and district champion but didn't place in the state tournament. He enrolled at Ohio State without ever talking to Russ, and walked on the team, but quit right away, feeling out of place. Then, over the next couple of months, he grew encouraged to try again. One day he worked out with Oklahoma State's Jason Allen at his high school, and

Allen told him he had what it took. Then Russ was at his daughters' school one day when Dan was working out there, and told Dan that he had spots in the lineup. Dan came back to the team, and started for his last two years.

As a senior he was seeded sixth at 158 in the Big Ten tournament. He started out by beating the top seed. He ended up sixth, after all, and qualified for the NCAA tournament.

Dan won on conditioning. He could take anybody down at the end of a match, when he still had energy left. "I think I can take anybody down, the way you think you can turn anybody once you're on top," he says. We worked each other, made each other better. Dan, Rob and I had an un-spoken competition to see who could do better — in a healthy way.

Rob and I used to marvel at how Dan could eat so poorly and still be able to withstand training sessions as if they were a walk in the park. One morning a week before the Big Tens, we came home from a morning run. Rob and I quickly went for our Gatorade, followed by oatmeal and ba-nanas. When we walked into the living room, we found Dan eating pret-

Trying to turn Iowa State's Barry Weldon, 1997 NCAA final

zels and drinking Coca Cola. We said, laughing, "What are you doing?" He replied, "Hey, breakfast of champions." From then on we called him Grandpa because he never got emotional or excited about anything, and I swear his heart rate was the same when he was lying on the couch as it was after a match. He was always my roommate on the road, and I called him my good luck charm. He, in my book, is like Rudy, the diminutive football player for Notre Dame who finally gets to play in the last game of his senior year. Dan's the Rudy of wrestling. I was so proud of him when he made his goal of being a national qualifier.

I was seeded fourth for the 1997 NCAA Championships at Northern Iowa and ended up in the final, opening with two pins and then getting decisions in the quarterfinal against Edinboro's 12th-seeded Jim Straight and the semifinal against Lehigh's unseeded John Van Doren.

So there I was, in the championship bout, at the center of what I call the glory: cameras, bright lights, roaring crowds, ESPN thrusting a microphone in your face, all the pressure you could imagine. I tried to soak in the atmosphere. I'd already gotten farther than expected. I looked at the elevated mat, and the photographers all around me, and I didn't get in The Zone.

I lost to Iowa State's Barry Weldon, 6–2. He was the second seed, a powerful man, and he knew how to exploit my weaknesses.

I was thrilled to be an All-American, but I wondered if I'd always be a bridesmaid, always second place. What, I wondered, did I need to do to prepare? To reach the goals I'd set?

It was hard to feel too happy even about placing second. Four Ohio State wrestlers had qualified, three of us had been seeded and only one of us had placed. The other three Buckeyes — Anthony Gary, Nick Nutter and Jeff Bucher — were all one match away from All-American status. The silence in the car on the way home was an intense reminder of how much Russ — and we — expected.

Chapter Fourteen

The Pressure of Being the Favorite

(Mitch)

I entered my final season as the favorite to win the national championship. I was ranked number one from the beginning, stayed there over the months that followed. So I want to start this last chapter of my career with thoughts for all of you who face the pressures of being ranked.

Rankings are good for a sport. They keep people involved and interested. They also create a goal for an athlete — if you're rated number nine, you want to be in the top five.

When I was ranked number one, I had to be ready for every match, because guys were gunning for me. I also had the feeling that if I lost, it would feel like the end of the world. Once you're at the top, your wish to stay there is very motivating. You don't want to settle for less. Unfortunately, I used to stay up at night and wonder who could beat me. What if, what if. It kept me from improving. I'd get a lead on an opponent and hang on. I didn't want to lose that top ranking. But then I'd say, "I have to stop this, I won't win a national title this way." Maybe that's why I had only seven pins that final year, when I had 16 the year before. I wouldn't take chances. Plus, people picked neutral on me, so I couldn't pin them.

My goal was to be number one. I wouldn't settle for less. But the whole thing caused me some serious stress. I couldn't sleep. Even more, I wanted to go undefeated and untied, the way Rex Holman had in 1992–93, the only guy in Ohio State history to do it. It would've been nice, but maybe it was too much. Maybe I willed myself into losing that one match that season, to Jevon Herman of Illinois in my last home dual meet.

I talked to Rex all season about it. He'd say, "Don't worry about rankings, you're still the best guy at 177." It was good advice, but easier said than done. I talked to people back in Canton about the pressures on me — Neal Riggs, Rick Cassara. They'd remind me that rankings didn't matter, all that mattered was who won at the end. I tried to listen. I even considered meeting with the OSU sports psychologist because I was such a basket case. Instead I followed the advice of my father, "return to the basics — the fundamental strengths of my style."

Before the season began, it almost ended.

I wanted badly to improve my takedown techniques, so I went to a national training camp in Colorado the summer before my senior year. And I suffered a partial tear to a major ligament in my right knee, the LCL. It wasn't as serious as tearing the ACL, but it was bad. I was training with Les Gutches, a former NCAA champion who was a member of the World Team, and 30 seconds into our match he pinned my knee to the mat and lifted up on my ankle.

Six weeks later, I couldn't bend my knee 90 degrees. I thought my season was over, because surgery seemed the most likely solution, and I never would've recovered in time.

I went to Columbus to see Dr. John Lombardo, the Ohio State athletics physician. Instead I ended up seeing his assistant, Dr. Andrew Cosgarea. Dr. Cosgarea, who is now at Johns Hopkins University, had just written a paper that said knees were being operated on too often. He

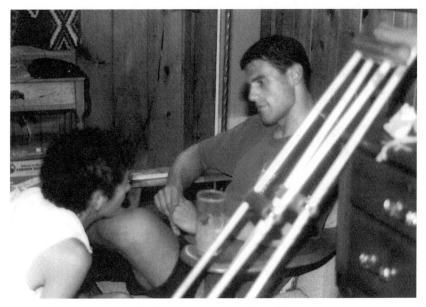

A little encouragement from Mom

told my dad that if he operated on me, I might be able to wrestle by the end of the season or I might not. The doctor decided to let my knee heal on its own, and he decided to brace it so I couldn't move it, which was counter to what most doctors did.

Three months later, in early December, I won the Las Vegas Invitational.

I was miserable for those three months — moody, frustrated, irritable. Anyone who has been injured and can't take part in his sport knows the feeling. It jeopardized my relationships with the people I cared about. I was able to work my upper body, and I attacked the Upper Body Ergometer (UBE) machine in our practice room to the point where I practically broke it. A family friend who was a trainer later told my parents that my knee injury won me the championship, because it made me focus on the task at hand — getting back into action.

Vince O'Brien, our team's trainer that year, says the LCL injury is especially tough for wrestlers, who rely so much on their knee strength and on being able to take the shock of having an opponent shoot in on them. He thinks surgery, besides keeping me idle until January, wouldn't have guaranteed that I'd return to action. He agrees that my focus on other aspects of my body, such as my upper body, during that time helped. "Nine out of ten times, I know if someone is going to make it back [into competition] after an injury," he says. "I thought you were questionable. I was surprised, and I think if we'd had surgery, it wouldn't have had this result."

My sister Sarah had ACL surgery before her swimming season when she was a sophomore at St. Lawrence in 1998–99. She told Scott, my co-author, that one day that January she was in the training room for three hours, and "I kept thinking of Mitch and how it [the knee injury and rehabilitation] made him stronger. I remember how tough it made him."

At Las Vegas, I wore a brace on my left knee, the healthy one, because I knew opponents would crank on my hurting knee. In the finals I defeated an old rival, Aaron Simpson of Arizona State.

I would tell younger guys that injuries are hard to deal with but don't rush back into action, no matter how much your coach wants you to. Your body will tell you when. But do everything possible in rehab and outside of it. Push yourself. It's the only thing you can focus on; the rest is out of your control.

My recovery was miraculous. My knee was never a factor again.

Chapter   Fourteen

That first semester, those three college wrestlers died while cutting weight, a tragedy that changed our sport. It scared my teammates and me badly, because we'd all been doing what one of the kids, Jeff Reese of Michigan, had been doing when he died. Dan DiCesare, our 158-pounder who lived with me, had cut weight at times to the point where his legs went numb. I'd cut weight to the point where I had to rest after walking 10 steps.

We all felt so bad for the guys, for their coaches. Russ said if it ever happened to him, if he lost any of us because of weight loss, he'd quit the sport. He told us not to use Creatine to build muscle, though of course we had been using it.

We didn't know what to think. I thought there was a chance the NCAA would certify everybody then, in the first semester, and I'd have to wrestle at 197. Some guys hadn't gone down yet. It didn't happen, though. Russ wrote down our weights before and after practice, monitoring us.

We were afraid wrestling would be probed and turned inside out after the deaths, and that seemed awful, since wrestling doesn't get much press in the best of circumstances. Reporters from television shows such as 20/20 showed up for weigh-ins at tournaments, interviewing random wrestlers who had dropped pounds to make weight. I was concerned about a rumor that the season might be terminated to avoid more deaths.

For the first time since I'd known him, Russ said "okay" if a guy on the team said he didn't want to cut weight.

The NCAA didn't change the setup for tournament weigh-ins until the next season, which helped me. I was good at pulling weight for the weigh-in before the first day of a tournament. I could still go up in weight and keep it there for the second and third days.

The season unfolded gradually. Victory followed victory.

Now I was a senior, a guy everyone on the team looked to for leadership. At times it got to be too much. Russ Hellickson would tell the team, "Mitch is the only one who's working." He'd highlight me after every match. I didn't feel I deserved it, because some guys were working harder than I was, but I was wearing people down where other guys weren't. The team grew frustrated and, unfortunately, after the Christmas break nobody really improved.

The tension grew. I finally stood up in front of the team one day, when Russ wasn't there, and said, "I'm sorry Coach keeps highlighting me, but some people could work harder and show a little more fight in their matches."

Certain teammates were special to me. Rob Archer and Dan DiCesare were my housemates again, sharing my life. Another teammate moved in after he and his roommates were robbed at gunpoint in their apartment: Pete Rogers, a sophomore 150-pounder from Wisconsin.

Pete reminded me of myself at a younger age, a country boy in the big city. And he's built the way I am, long and lean. I call him one of "my boys" among the Buckeyes.

Pete grew up outside of a town called Oostburg, on a farm, with five brothers and five sisters. He's the youngest. His father, Al, drowned while ice fishing when Pete was in ninth grade, and for a while he was the only one home with his mother, Faye. One of his older brothers coached him in high school, and Pete was a three-time Wisconsin state champion. He missed home like crazy when he first got to Ohio State. By now he's gotten used to the urban setting, but he figures he'll go back home when he's done.

I tried to work with him that season and then in 1998–99, when he started at 165 pounds, taking over Dan's spot. Pete and I are a lot alike, and I try to teach him my funky moves. It's gone well; he won 13 in a row at one point in '98–'99, and qualified for the NCAA Championships. I've tried to help him be more confident.

Matt Fratta and Jeff Bucher were two more of "my boys" on the team.

In Matt's case it was partly because we shared spirituality. He belonged to Athletes in Action, a Christian brotherhood of college athletes.

Matt split time at 118 pounds as a junior, when I was a senior, and started at 125 pounds the next season. Matt's from Willard, Ohio, and like me he was a wrestler at a high school that valued other sports more, basketball in his case. Like me, and Archer and Nutter and Pete Rogers, he was coached by a relative; his dad was an assistant coach for his high school team. Matt went to Hofstra University on Long Island first, wanting to get away from the Midwest, but transferred to Ohio State after one season.

I thought of Matt as a kindred spirit because he loved wrestling as a source of discipline and relished our sport's uniqueness. We savored the times when other athletes said they couldn't endure our workouts or imagine competing alone in front of a crowd. Matt was just as proud of the way he balanced sport with school. He was an industrial and systems engineering major, so his workload was intense. He thinks the two things gave his life harmony.

Jeff was our 142-pounder when I was a senior, the stocky-strong kind of wrestler, just a rock. He was Big Ten runner-up at 134 the year before, as a sophomore, losing by 13 points to Mark Ironside, the national champion from Iowa. Jeff met up with Ironside again in the NCAA quarterfinals, and this time the story was different — Jeff lost by 9–8. He ended up qualifying for the NCAA Championships three times. He was so tough, and I badly wanted him to get All-American status before his career ended, but that eluded him.

Jeff's stories of growing up struck a chord in me. He had two brothers who were 17 and 18 when he was 8 years old, and they used to make him run at them while they pushed him down. He just kept coming. It reminds me of those older boys beating on me during practice at Canton.

When he carried out the trash for his parents, Jeff used to carry all the trash bags at once and run, sprint. He says he was too lazy to carry them two at a time. That's not my idea of laziness.

In early February I wrestled in the All-Star Classic in Buffalo, a rare chance to compete in my home state. I had a lot to prove on my home turf. I beat John Van Doren of Lehigh by one point. The next day I became very ill with the flu and missed eight or nine days, just as I was training for the Big Ten tournament. My mom had it too, at the same time, and it took a lot out of her. The flu caused me to lose so much weight, I actually was a natural 177. I wrestled a couple of times, but my strength was pretty low. I wanted the season to be over. Finally, the pressure was getting to me. For a full week I lay in bed, mentally and physically broken.

I was still undefeated, but I was feeling it all close in. I snapped during morning runs. I'd be swearing before practice started.

My last home match arrived, Sunday, February 22, 1998, a Big Ten match against Illinois. It was Senior Day not just for me but for the others who were bowing out, including Rob and Dan. Russ wasn't sure I should wrestle. Unbeknownst to me, my parents were coming, the first time they'd seen me wrestle in an Ohio State home meet — they'd always seen me on the road.

Jevon Herman beat me, mauled me. I'd defeated him five times in a row, including the Big Ten title bout in 1997, but this time everything came down on me — my illness, the top ranking, the pressure of being undefeated. Rob said later that I looked not just like I was sick but ready to quit wrestling.

I didn't take it well. I lashed out at my parents. Mom had a half hour talk with me. She said I had to get right with God, I had to be humble. And I agreed. I began to rely on God's support and guidance. I ate a lot, I got the weight back.

A week before the Big Ten tournament, Russ said I looked down, as if maybe I was done with wrestling, with trying. "You know what you've got to do, to prepare," he said. "If you just want to wrestle one match at practice and leave, you can." He structured practice around what the guys needed, and that wasn't like him. Our schedule had been so brutal that season, because he wanted to simulate high-level tournament competition. He backed off.

I was seeded second behind Herman in the Big Ten tournament. I won by pin in my first match and then decisioned Rob Neidlinger of Penn State in the semifinals, 7–2. I squared off against Herman again in the final and won, 4–0.

My friend Wess Audsley says that winning two Big Ten titles is equal to winning a national title. The league is that impressive.

But something else happened the day I reached the Big Ten final.

After my win over Neidlinger, I got a call at the hotel from my family. They were in Syracuse for the New York State high school championships. My brother Johnny, who had placed fifth as a sophomore, had reached the state final this time, as a junior. Just as I had.

They put Johnny on and he said, "Well, I didn't wrestle so good. I made some mistakes." And I said, "Don't worry about it." I didn't know whether he'd won or lost.

"Well, it felt good to win it," he said finally.

It sank in. I was so overjoyed.

My brother was the state champion at 145, the first state champion from our section.

He'd succeeded where I had failed. I should've known.

♎

Johnny

(Mitch)

Johnny was afraid I'd be jealous, when he told me that he was the 1998 New York State champion at 145 pounds.

I was not. I had said, five years earlier, that if I couldn't be state champion, I hoped my brother would be.

I just wished I could have seen it, instead of being a few hours away, at Penn State for the Big Ten tournament. I think I saw him wrestle twice while he was in high school.

Johnny is five years younger than I am, so we never got to wrestle on the same team. The best we could do was wrestle at home. We had a game over the years, where I'd sit on the floor and he'd attack me. I could only use my legs, while he could wrestle with arms and legs. I'm several inches taller, so my long legs made for a nice opponent for him. I feel that was one of the reasons why I was able to use proper leg and hip positioning, beyond the average wrestler.

Johnny is quieter than I am, polite to a fault, and very spiritual. When he wins, he clasps his hands and looks skyward in thanks. He likes helping others. In high school he worked at a center for mentally handicapped, helping people in any way he could. He's calm and collected, though like me he worries about every opponent.

He also is far more gifted as an athlete than I am. It comes so easily for him that he doesn't have to work as hard as I did, and I tell him constantly to work, to be hungry, as I was. He listens sometimes, and he trains pretty hard, but in high school he enjoyed much more of a social life than I did when I was his age.

"I love wrestling, and I work hard at it, but it's not my life as it was for Mitch," he likes to say.

And when he gets into a match, his eyes take on this look, this deep, hard intensity, and he curls his tongue and bites it, and you know the other guy is in trouble.

Johnny almost didn't wrestle in high school, he was so leery of being "Mitch Clark's brother" and trying to follow what I'd accomplished. True, he grew up with the sport; Dad made sure of it. But Johnny liked hockey too. In sixth grade, he had to choose. He decided to wrestle, but he almost chose hockey. There was a huge battle between my father and Canton's hockey coaches. Thank God he won.

Johnny likes to wear down opponents with shoulder shots, fakes, grinding. Some opponents get very rattled by it.

Johnny placed fifth in the state at 140 as a 10th grader. As a junior he was, like me, a surprise finalist. He and Coach Neal Riggs were giddy at being there, on that center mat, while the whole Onondaga County War Memorial crowd looked on.

Johnny honors Section X after becoming its first New York State champion

He beat a kid from the section that stretches along the state's Southern Tier, from Binghamton to Ithaca and Elmira. The score was 5–4. My sister Nicki taught in the kid's school, knew him and said he was a nice guy.

Afterward Johnny disappeared for about 45 minutes, back into some area behind the stage, and cried, he was so overcome with joy.

"I was so thrilled, but I thought about what it would be like to be on the other side of that score," he says, "and I thought of Mitch." He thought of how I'd taken second twice.

Now he adds another spin to it.

"Mitch sets his goals so high that even when he underachieves, he achieves something," Johnny says. "Even when he finished second in the state, I'm not sure he realized how good that was, because his only goal was to be a state champ. So many people would love to be in the finals."

Johnny won another state title in 1999, at 152. He was now the dominant wrestler in our section. He still went to Montreal with Dad a couple of times a week, to face men. Unlike me, he got to wrestle on the same team with his younger brother, since Charlie was the 125-pounder as a seventh grader.

Johnny found it tough to be a defending champion at that level (he'd already been a defending champion of the section a couple of times). In the first two rounds he wrestled cautiously, in what's called "wrestling not to lose, not wrestling to win." Dad was annoyed. Johnny looked better in the semifinals, and in the finals he did what he had to.

By then, he'd already signed his letter of intent to wrestle for Ohio State. He'd be joining me in Columbus. I would be one of his coaches.

After Johnny's first state title, I had two weeks until the NCAA Championships. I was so proud and happy for him, and it made me all the more determined.

Chapter Sixteen

The Top of the Mountain

(Mitch)

Now, to use my father's favorite analogy, I was approaching the summit of the mountain I was climbing. There had been so many stages along the way, so many people who helped me push onward and then fell back while I trudged onward. In reality, of course, they were all going to be there at the NCAA Championships at Cleveland State University. I didn't know the scope of the crowd that would be cheering for me — Jerry Smilgin, my high school coach Neal Riggs, Wess Audsley, former and current teammates, and of course family galore. But this was the last approach to the top, with just a few people along: my coaches and teammates Dan DiCesare (sixth place in the Big Ten to qualify at 158) and Jeff Bucher (fifth place at 134). My father had gotten a photographer's pass, for the second year, and he sat at matside, trying to keep quiet (NCAA rules prohibit anything resembling cheering by the news media). Mom was up there in the crowd. And God was there.

I'd begun to realize that getting hurt, getting ill and losing to Jevon Herman were maybe signs that I needed to be more humble if I wanted to reach my goal. That last weekend, Mom reminded me even more of how important it was to remember my spiritual side.

My favorite saying had always been "I can do all things through Christ, which strengthens me," Phillippians 4:13.

Dad gave me Mark 11:24, which read, "Therefore I say to you, what things soever you desire, when you pray, believe that you will receive them, and you shall have them."

Mom told me, one night before I went to the tournament, that she had known Johnny would win the state title, and she knew as certainly that I'd win the national title. "Ma," I said, "how can you make such a claim, when I have so much wrestling to do?" But she said she knew. I was so shocked that she'd go out on a limb like that. I was angry. Here I had five tough opponents ahead of me, and she was putting pressure on me.

All season, I'd been eating vitamins and Power Gels and Power Bars before matches, to help me keep my energy level up. Fifteen or 20 minutes before a bout, I'd have two Power Gels. It was Dad's idea; he'd begun eating them because he'd become a marathon runner.

During the season I also had a designer protein shake and multiple vitamins on a regular basis.

Between rounds of that NCAA tournament, I ate a lot of pasta.

As usual I had trouble in the first match. I always gave up the first points in the opening bout. But I beat Doug Lee of Oregon, 12–5. Then I pinned Dave Murray of Lock Haven in 4:04.

Jeff lost his first bout by one point, then won his first two consolation bouts. But he got pinned and was out of the tournament.

Dan lost his first bout, also by one point, 2–1, to the ninth seed. His first consolation bout was against the eighth seed, Josh Holiday of Minnesota. Dan had upset him in the Big Ten's first round, 4–3, when Holiday was the top seed and Dan wasn't seeded at all. They had another tight match and Holiday prevailed, 3–1. My buddy Dan's career was over.

But, as I said earlier in this story, during a tournament you have to focus on yourself as much as you can. Sure, keep an eye on your teammates, but avoid watching too many matches or worrying about them too much. It'll take the edge right off your focus.

I needed all of the focus I could muster. My quarterfinal opponent was Rob Neidlinger of Penn State.

I'd sensed this was coming since I saw Neidlinger's name in my bracket. He was seeded ninth. I'd defeated him twice that season, by 3–1 in the dual meet and then by 7–2 in the Big Ten semifinals. Getting a third victory over him would be difficult, because he'd been figuring out my style.

Neidlinger was a guy after my own heart, a walk-on from Big Spring High School in Carlisle, Pa., who had claimed a spot in the lineup of one of the nation's better teams. Like me, he'd dreamed of being a state champion in high school, only to fail, losing in the semifinals as a senior and placing fifth. He'd wrestled at 190 for Penn State in 1996–97, placing third in the Big Ten. Now he'd dropped to 177. John Fritz, the Nittany Lions' head coach, said in a press guide on the Web that the move was "a real sacrifice. It shows a special part about what it's worth to Rob and his dedication to it."

Scoring a "go ahead" takedown against Neidlinger in last 15 seconds

To win, I needed to stay ahead of him, because he was so good on his feet that if he got ahead, I'd have a hard time coming back against his defensive moves.

When I called my family's hotel the night before the quarterfinals, everyone was having a party. Their lives were carefree, and I envied them. I was very, very nervous for this match, and that wasn't like me.

Neidlinger had a 4–2 lead in the third period.

I remember that, with 30 seconds to go and behind by two points, I asked myself why this was happening. I almost felt deceived. I thought of Mom's words before the tournament.

Not a second later, the referee called Neidlinger for locking his hands.

The referee gave me a point. I escaped to make the score 4–4.

Then I scored a defensive takedown with seven seconds left and won, 6–4.

And I knew I'd be the national champion. It was like a big weight off my chest.

I climbed up into the stands. My contingent of family and friends was shell-shocked and drained. Some of my friends had arrived just as my match was underway. They thought that before they even put their bags down, I'd be in the loser's bracket. It was all so exciting, the semifinal bout seemed anticlimactic. I defeated fifth-seeded John Withrow of Pitt by 5–0 to reach the final for the second time.

Coach Fritz and Neidlinger both told the press that he hadn't locked his hands, he'd gripped my ankle with one hand and my knee with the other. Coach Fritz said Neidlinger out-wrestled me. John Lange, Penn State's Big Ten champion at 158, said the referee was in a bad position to make that call.

Dad believes I would've found a way to win, even if Neidlinger had gone ahead, 6–2. I don't think about it. I just accept what did happen.

Staying on top of Pitt's John Withrow in the 1998 NCAA semifinal

Chapter   Sixteen

Dan and I were roommates at the hotel. It was pretty neat to wake up that morning, March 21, 1998, and say, "I'm going to wrestle for the national championship tonight."

I shopped with my family, and got a massage and chiropractic work from Kevin Coloton, a high school buddy who was now a physical therapist at Johns Hopkins Hospital. And on the way to Cleveland State's arena with my coaches, flipping the radio dial, we heard Mariah Carey singing our Ohio State team anthem, "Make It Happen." She hit that phrase about getting down on your knees and praying to the Lord, and He's going to make it happen — and I just knew.

Mom surprised me by approaching as I warmed up. She never did that. She always passed her Scripture phrases to me through someone else. But she'd been reading the Bible for two hours early that morning, and she was convinced I'd win, and she was determined to see me. Mom gave me two verses from Psalm 20, written on her hotel stationery:

> *May He give you the desire of your heart*
> *and make all your plans succeed.*
> *We will shout for joy when you are victorious*
> *and lift up our banner in the name of God.*

It goes on to say that God is with me, surrounding me. I thanked her and returned to the process of getting in The Zone.

I have to thank our team trainers, Vince O'Brien and Don Sherwood, for spending time with me in an isolated room before the match, talking to me about anything. I saw through what they were trying to do: distract me from the pressure. It helped, but I still can't believe I didn't crack under the pressure I had put on myself.

I've never talked to Vertus Jones, the sophomore from West Virginia who was my opponent in the finals, the last man between me and my dream. As a sophomore, and as the sixth seed, he was probably thrilled to be in the championship bout, as I was the year before.

I was so deeply in The Zone that I remember nothing about that match. On the videotape, I see Jones get behind me but not attempt a takedown as we go out of bounds. Then I take him down for a five-point move and keep cranking him until I win by technical fall, 18–0, as time expires in the first period. Then I see myself stand up and point skyward, then point to my family and friends and the Ohio State crowd. Then I walk around like a robot, still in The Zone, not hugging my coaches — which I deeply regret — and telling the ESPN interviewer, former Olympic gold medalist Jeff Blatnick, about trying to avoid the glory (the distractions of being in the finals). At one point emotion wells up in me so fast that I start to cry, then I concentrate on what he's asking me. To some basic question about what I was doing in the match, I told him, "Once you break someone, and they're mentally broken . . . He was going down and I was going up."

At the end, I thought about Johnny's state title and said, "It's been a good year for the Clark family, that's for sure."

Mitch has Jones in trouble early in the NCAA finals

Nick Nutter says the crowd was quiet, stunned, because the match was over so quickly. They'd just seen this entertaining final at 167 pounds, won by Iowa's Joe Williams, and then my match was over before they knew it. Jeff Bucher says he almost felt robbed. He stared out at the mat and said, "What happened out there?" He says he often had that feeling when he watched me wrestle anyway. Rob Archer remembers thinking before the match, "If Mitch does his crazy stuff, Jones won't know what hit him." Rob says my crowd never sat down once the bout started, and he was crying for me afterward. Wess Audsley sat there and thought,

"Will I ever know a kid in that way again?" because he'd watched me grow up.

I remember two things: staring at the cracks in the floor while I waited to be called to the victory stand, and looking down from the stand at a

At last . . . an NCAA Champion

television reporter and thinking she had the strangest shoes. That night, at our celebration party, I alluded to the thoughts I had while on the victory stand. My friend Dave McLean later told me it was hilarious because everyone wants to know what thoughts of joy you have while on that stand, and all I could think about were those white orthopedic shoes. It goes to show you that once you get into The Zone, it's not easy to change gears even hours later.

The party in my family's hotel suite seemed to go on forever that night. I had to thank everybody for being there and for what they'd done for me. I was so relieved, to finally reach that major goal.

I hugged Rob Archer and he said, "That was a storybook ending, just perfect."

Several of my father's St. Lawrence wrestlers from over the years were there. One of them, Jim Townsend, Class of 1983, had flown in from California, where he's a film producer; while wrestling for SLU, he'd been noticed by a modeling agency, had gone into modeling and then acting. Dave Hudson, heavyweight in the Class of 1980, who had succeeded Dad as St. Lawrence's coach, was there from Governor Dummer Academy in Massachusetts, where he was athletic director. Mike Conners, 1984 NCAA Division III champion at heavyweight, was there; he was now the football and wrestling coach at Dad's high school, Fulton. John

Clark family celebrating Mitch's championship title in Cleveland

Canty, 1988 NCAA Division III runner-up at 118, part of Dad's 1988 national championship team, was there. And other people: Kevin Coloton, my high school friend who had given me the massage; Nate Hinesman, a friend from my freshman dorm; Ken and Beth Reger, longtime friends from Trout Lake; and Leigh Cassara, ex-girlfriend and soulmate from home.

And of course Dave McLean had shocked me by flying in from Scotland, where he was in graduate school. My oldest sister Christy and her husband, and my next-oldest sister Nicki and her future husband, were there, as were my other two sisters and two brothers, parents, uncle, cousin, and other friends.

Wess says I paid attention to everybody, "almost as if there were 50 people on the victory stand with you. You made us all feel like part of it. I can go to the NCAAs (over the years) and see that in one of 20 champions. Most of them just think of themselves."

But why wouldn't I be sure to include everybody? Everybody at that party had in some way helped me climb that mountain.

Part II

Technique and Training

The   Scramble

Ever since I was a kid, I've had a competitive soul. I used to play games with my other siblings, usually ones we made up, simple in form and strategy. Whether it was who could throw the rock against the barn or who could catch the others, I had to win. I couldn't stand to lose, and if I did, my temper flared, resulting in a fit of rage that sent my brothers and sisters running for cover.

I brought that same competitive edge to the wrestling mat. That is probably one of the best assets I possess. In the wrestling room, it's all about pride. Even in my training sessions, when my workout partners would score on me, I felt it a necessity to quickly score the next point and punish them for scoring on me. Every wrestler needs to obtain this attitude, one that conveys, "Don't you dare score on me again." Certainly guys have turned around and scored on me again, but they had to work real hard to do it. If two wrestlers have that attitude in practice, they will get the best out of each other, because neither one wants to give up anything. They'll simulate a pace close to what a real match's pace would be, which will inevitably bring them to top-notch conditioning. Those who get scored on, and then lie on the mat feeling sorry for themselves before they attempt their next move, don't have enough pride and will never get into competitive shape.

In the practice room at Ohio State, guys will be screaming with anger at getting beaten up. But they will always turn around and get more physical, or pick it up to another level to even the score. Often it ends in a two-man brawl where technique is no longer used, the adrenaline takes over and you rely on sheer horsepower. At the end of the flurry, two tired warriors will lie on the mat, both unable to get up, but one of those guys scored the last critical takedown because he didn't break first. Either way, they both benefit from their hustle and their refusal to get taken down.

"Mitch Is Mitch"
Scrambling leads to takedown in opening period, 1998 Big Ten final

One of the best ways I found to survive, when I was a freshman in a Division I wrestling room, was to constantly "scramble" in every position. Scrambling is a generic term for constantly moving and never giving up on any position. It requires grit, strategy and conditioning.

I first learned to scramble at the Montreal Wrestling Club, where day in and day out I was getting mauled by higher-class wrestlers. It came to a point where I would have to find justice in spreading out the time it took for them to score each takedown on me. Not by stalling or backing away, but by fending them off with everything I could muster. Maybe it meant that at the last second I had to dive between their legs as they were taking me to the mat, or do the splits when they attempted to finish a single-leg, or adjust my body just as they were going to cover me for a takedown.

Unless it meant I was going to give up back points, I wouldn't give up on any position. Believe me, that can often frustrate an opponent, because most wrestlers tend to relax for a second once they think they have the takedown. I believe you should gain back your position in that moment of hesitation, then quickly take advantage of your opponent's frustration. Opponents would tire because I was always moving and because I was used to the pace of long scrambles or flurries.

I can honestly say that I rarely scored off my first maneuver. It was the third, fourth or maybe fifth adjustment I made during a series or flurry that would gain me points. And usually it was because the guy was mentally broken or fatigued.

So, if you are constantly getting mauled by your opponent, have someone take a stopwatch and record how long you have spread out their takedowns on you. Chances are, if it means something to you, you will find a way to increase his time between takedowns and eventually you might get the best of him.

The keys to being a good scrambler:

1. flexibility
2. hip awareness
3. good conditioning
4. savvy

Flexibility is somewhat controlled by your genetics. One can, however, work on this area. Stretching after each training session, especially after weight lifting, can increase flexibility and decrease injuries. Being flexible allows you to slither out of your opponent's control or test his ability to execute a move to perfection.

Hip awareness involves knowing how and when to shift your hips to counter a takedown. For instance, if a man is bringing me to the mat and I'm falling, I tuck my head and roll underneath his legs. The ad-

Flexibility, hip awareness, and savvy

Creating an opening at the beginning of a scramble

justments he makes will be the deciding factor in how I move my hips. If he settles his hips and falls on me, I must switch to one leg, hip over to my stomach and elevate, bringing my hips under once again. Four adjustments are made with my hips in as many seconds.

Conditioning can't be emphasized enough. During the heart of the season my coaches have always stressed interval training. That is exactly what wrestling consists of: a hard 30-second flurry, followed by a 10-to-15-second break (perhaps walking back to center mat). That is exactly why I trained by pushing a car 50 yards, resting and driving while my partner pushed it back. My heart rate would go sky high after that push. It would be a full-body workout: triceps, shoulders, hips, quads and calves. But I would be able to bring my heart rate back down while my partner was pushing. I believe that is why I outlasted my opponents on a scramble, because I was relentless with my adjustments and motion due to my training. Yes, I would feel like I hit a semi truck after pushing cars or completing a tough scramble. But I conditioned my body to recover at a faster rate. Instead of needing 20 seconds to bring my heart rate down, I needed only 10 seconds.

Savvy is acquired by being in certain positions so many times that your motion becomes automatic regardless of the opponent's reactions. You know that you possess this if you can wrestle and score in positions while blindfolded. Also, being savvy can mean that you have a few tricks in your bag, ones that work on almost anyone and will bail you out of trouble. I won a national championship because I was savvy, unique in my own style. You need to have moves that throw opponents off, however funky or unorthodox they may be. I'm not saying the fundamentals aren't important, but do not fall prey to becoming a one-dimensional or textbook wrestler.

The   Zone

I've talked a little about being in "The Zone" when I wrestle. I guess the way to express it is, you just get into a frame of mind where your body takes over with what it's been conditioned to do, what you've been trained to do by those years of practice.

"Getting into the Zone"

You don't think about moves, really. If you think, "I'm going to go for this move now," you're not in The Zone. You have to be in a state where you know what you're going to do two moves before you do it. You just get on a roll, you absorb what's going on around you without being fully aware of it and you start trusting in yourself. You get in tune with your ability.

It's almost as if you want to be the center of attention, you want everyone to watch you. In the parade of finalists before the NCAA championship matches, for example, I felt it: "Watch me, see what I'm going to do."

I focus so hard, I rarely hear anything beyond the mat during a bout. Once in a while, I can hear the announcer listing my accomplishments. But that's it.

I've been asked if everything slows down around me. The answer is no, but it's as if I watch myself wrestle. This sounds silly, but it's almost an out of body experience.

I was in The Zone throughout my junior season at Ohio State, until the NCAA final against Barry Weldon of Iowa State. I wasn't in it when I faced him, I was too distracted by the crowd and the photographers and the atmosphere.

But it's tough to get into The Zone for 42 matches out of the year anyway.

As I've said, I can't remember a thing about the 1998 NCAA title bout. It's kind of too bad, because it was the best feeling of my life, but I don't recall a single thing. The only memories I have are from what I see on the videotape. I believe I got into The Zone and then remained in it after the match ended, because I was geared to go three periods and it finished after only one. Even an hour later, while I was on the medal stand, I was looking down at that woman reporter's shoes, totally oblivious to the fact that I'm on top of the awards stand and 13,000 people are staring at me. Not even close to thinking about that.

To young wrestlers, I would say don't try to get in The Zone for every match, because you'll wear yourself out. You have to know what matches to get "up" for. You'll spread yourself thin. It'll be too much for you. You've got to be one of those people who, when the light's on and the time's right, you'll know when to do it.

Chapter Nineteen

Thoughts and Advice from a Champion

You're known in the wrestling community as a pinner. Is that a frame of mind or something technical you learned?

I just honestly wanted to get the match over with. I thought maybe I didn't want to go six minutes, and this was the easiest way to get off the mat and score a lot of points for my team. When I get the guy near his back, I think, "This is my golden opportunity, don't let this one go, just don't let him off his back." Once he's there, I would wrap him up as if I were a python.

When do you think young wrestlers should think about using legs?

I learned about legs primarily in college, though I did use legs in high school but didn't score with them most of the time. I think anytime a wrestler starts to go in the weight room and do squats and lunges, build up their hips and legs, it's time to learn. But learn how to ride and break guys down first. Then, as soon as the fundamentals on top are learned, get right into legs.

Coaches sometimes shy away from encouraging kids to use legs too early because they end up just clinging to their opponent and not being a pinner. What do you think?

I agree they have to learn the proper technique early. If they learn cross-body rides, they're going to be a rider. And they'll revert back to their roots, to what they learned as peewees, to throw in the legs and do an offensive leg turn. Then they'll be plenty apt to throw in legs later in their career.

A lot of times, because of takedowns, you got behind in matches. Does that bother you?

Not at all. At one point, that was my offense: if someone took me down, I reversed him. Then people started taking me down and letting me up. In fact, most of the time, guys took me down first, and then I'd get a quick reversal or just come back and get the next point. Whatever I do in the first period, I can make up for by taking top. I hardly ever panicked.

If you were down four points, would that bother you?

No. I knew I could score points in 30 seconds if I put my mind to it. I would never panic. As to my coaches, I'd always look in the corner and they knew what I was doing. I always thought, "Even if he takes me down three more times, I can always take top and pin him."

Do you always take top? When don't you?

I don't if it's a real close match, and I know the guy, and every point matters. He could stall and have me not turn him, and I need that one point. Then, I'll pick down. If I'm losing by a lot, I'll take top. If I'm winning by a lot, I'll take top, because I know I can ride him. Or, I'll take top if I think I can turn him pretty easily. So, 70 percent of the time, I take top.

What do you think about before a match? Is there a physical and mental warmup?

Basically, I try to simulate a match. When I go out and wrestle, I don't want it to be a shock. I want my body primed so that it's conditioned to wrestle. If I don't warm up, it'll tire me out a lot quicker in the match because my muscles won't be ready. It'll just be too much of a surprise.

How do you prepare yourself physically?

It varies. Just bang heads. Scrimmage with somebody, do calisthenics, just constant motion. As long as I was breaking a sweat, but not sweating. That's a wive's tale, that you have to be sweating when you go out.

Mentally?

With a lot of tournaments, half an hour before a match you feel your heart pounding through your chest. You start shaking. That's when you have to control your heart rate. It means your body is working hard and you'll tire yourself out. You have to bring your heart rate down. Mentally, I like to play games with myself. I'll say, "C'mon, in the scheme of things, this isn't a big deal."

Your father once asked you about getting "up" for matches. You just kind of looked at him.

He asked, "Why aren't you going to get warmed up and get pumped up?" He said some guys slap each other, that kind of thing. I wasn't into it. I told him, "I know what I have to do when I go out there." It's different for everyone. I'm not the kind of guy who jumps around and goes nuts. But there are some people who do it and need to do it.

Was weight training a big part of your life?

Yes, but outside the season. The incredible strength I developed from training with weights made a significant impact on my wrestling career — first it gave me confidence and second the power to finish my moves. In high school, I was told not to lift during the season, and I didn't. You can lose 30 percent of your muscle during wrestling season, between not lifting, and cutting weight. But if you're in the weight room two to three times a week during the season, you'll only lose a little muscle, about five percent. And that would make a huge difference — in the third period, you'll be that much stronger.

What part of your body do you work on?

I tend to isolate a body part and just go with it, try to fatigue it as much as possible. One of the things I used to do, I moved into an apartment when I was a senior that had an old set of weights. They looked like they'd been there 10 years. I'd grab a weight and I'd do 25 dead lifts and then 25 shrugs. The next day, I'd feel like I tore something in my hamstrings. That soreness would make me feel good about what I'd done. I'd just say, I'm going to beat this muscle into oblivion. Choose a body part that isn't going to be strained in that day's practice. I'd say lift up until 36 hours before a match.

What do you do after a really tough practice or weight lifting session?

You've got to get food in your system within the hour, maybe 90 minutes. Any food, but you need carbohydrates and protein. A protein shake or another supplement drink is ideal for post-workout fueling.

When do you begin preparing mentally for the end of the season?

I'd say six weeks. But a lot of people train for the Big Ten tournament, for getting past it, so unfortunately sometimes you have to start eight weeks before the state or national tournament.

Do you train differently at the end of the season?

Russ Hellickson had us do "shark baits." A guy goes out there for nine minutes, and each minute a different guy goes in on him. It just breaks you down mentally, you just want to quit. You turn into a lunatic. You're being taken down by guys who couldn't score a takedown on you the whole season if they tried. If you've got pride, it's hard to swallow.

Do you scout opponents?

I ask my coach or teammates, did you ever see this guy wrestle, does he do anything I should know about? You should always scout opponents somewhat. I take into consideration the outstanding things they do, but that's it. I don't watch film of guys. Russ always said, "Just do what you do."

Are summer wrestling camps and clinics important?

I always thought if you got one move out of a clinic, one thing you could practice and use during the season, you got your money's worth.

You had a serious elbow injury in high school, a sternum injury, and then, in college, a knee injury. All have a common denominator: they could have been operated on and weren't. Today, everyone seems quick to get an injury operated on. What do you think?

I deal with injury better than a lot of people, so what I'm saying is biased. Some people's bodies don't heal as well from surgery. I think surgery should be a last-ditch solution, a last resort. In some cases, it's a must. But I found that in the time they said I'd start to recover and think about rehab, I was usually already in rehab. It's not always good to go against medical opinion, but in my mind I was doing the right thing. I felt good about how the injury was going.

How did your height help you and hurt you?

It hurt me because I didn't have a lot of power or speed. But I always thought being tall was an advantage. In order to be a great wrestler, you have to be better than everybody else at the basics, and I didn't do as well at the basics. I was good at what I did. I went a different route and got good at what I did.

Let's say you're a freshman in college, and you're not in the lineup. What do you tell the people back home, who remember you as a star?

What I can't stand is when people aren't in the lineup and lie about it. Go back home and tell 'em you're not in the lineup. You're not going to fool anybody. Tell people the truth. No matter what kind of athlete you were in high school, the transition to college is tough, mostly from a confidence standpoint.

You don't get much better in college, you get more confident. If you're not in the lineup, you must wait your turn. Don't expect to not be successful, and if you crack the lineup, don't say, "I'm a freshman, I won't be a national champ until my junior or senior year." You can't wait for the future. You've got to believe you can do it now. Sometimes you do your best as a freshman — you're new to the scene, you don't know who anybody is. In this case you have fun and enjoy being the underdog.

Say I'm a freshman on a college team, and I'm getting my butt kicked. What can I do?

That it's a good sign. You want to be wrestling with guys in the room who are kicking your butt. If you have any will or desire, you'll get better. If you're not being challenged or beaten on by the older guys, you will not improve.

Say I'm a freshman on a college team, and I have an even or losing record. What do I tell people?

That it says something about your team's schedule. The schedule should be tough. The people who plan your season have to clone what will happen at the end of the year, when you reach the conference and NCAA competitions. When I got to the NCAA tournament, it was just another tournament, because I'd been to other big competitions. My teammate Jeff Bucher always said he wasn't afraid to wrestle anyone who wasn't from the Big Ten.

Competition is just another source of improvement. You've got to stress the end of the year as a goal. People remember you if you win the Big Ten, not if you beat the kid from Michigan in a dual meet. I lost in my final home dual meet to Jevon Herman of Illinois, but I beat him in the Big Ten finals two weeks later. My Big Ten title is what people remember.

Most athletes have little quirks, routines they do before they compete. Do you?

In high school, before a soccer game, three of us would sing "Amazing Grace." Real quietly, on the field. Another thing, Nick Nutter used to always snap (irritate) me because he'd say, "Mitch, you've got to eat this or you won't win your next match." He'd have ice cream with pepper, and maple syrup and cottage cheese, all mixed together. I'd eat it, because he was so good at predicting how I'd do. I was afraid if I didn't eat it, I'd lose. He'd say, "Do this or you won't be an All-American." And I felt like I had to do whatever he said. I'd be done eating, and he'd want me to finish a piece of pizza. I'd feel like I had to, so I would. Now, during the last five minutes of a match, I take off one article of clothing per minute until I'm down to my singlet.

How would you like people to remember you?

Just that I tried to help the sport of wrestling out by being creative, scoring points, defying what others want to do. To have spectators enjoy our sport. I can't tell you how many times people said, "Thank you for paying for my ticket," meaning they had fun watching me and through that they enjoyed the sport.

*"Therefore I say to you, what things soever you desire, when you pray,
believe that you will receive them, and you shall have them."*

Mark 11:24

Afterword

In the summer following the NCAA Championships, I gave Mitch a photo album that I had compiled during that final season at Ohio State. It began with these words, which also apply to this book:

This album is about a year in your life — but more importantly about years of prayer, a wrestler's dream and determination, and how God works in our lives.

This special year began on a high and low — your Div. I final loss to Barry Weldon from Iowa State. Before that match, Mom passed you a passage from Isaiah where the Prophet talks about those who hope in the Lord:

They will soar on wings like eagles
They will run and not grow weary
They will walk and not be faint.

You had a good tournament and fought hard that night, but lost on a controversial referee's decision in the last few seconds. . . . God was working with you then in much the same way as in your high school finals defeats, last summer's knee injury, and your last home meet at Ohio State. The key to understanding all of this is found incredibly in the verses preceding the ones that Mom gave you:

Do you not know? Have you not heard?
The Lord is the everlasting God
The Creator of the ends of the earth.
He will not grow tired or weary
And His understanding no one can fathom.
He gives strength to the weary
And increases the power of the weak.
Even youths grow tired and weary
And young men stumble and fall;

Afterword

But those who hope in the Lord
Will renew their strength.

God has renewed your strength over and over again — it is true Mitch that both Mom and I knew that you would win the Championship. God's spirit began pouring out in our lives weeks before our journey to Cleveland. For us the whole experience was very meaningful. I want to tell you about another event that happened in the late 1970s right after you were born. Our star wrestler, Mitch Brown, competed at the Div. I Championships at the Myriad Center in Oklahoma City, Oklahoma. After Mitch lost, I watched the awards ceremony for his weight and wondered if I would ever have the opportunity to coach a Div. I All-American — little did I know that it would be another Mitch. By the way he lost to University of Wisconsin national champion Lee Kemp — Kemp was coached by Russ Hellickson.

My year following you around the country as a photographer produced two of my all-time favorite photographs — I've titled them "Getting into the Zone" and "Mitch Is Mitch" — both shots characterize what set you above all others. The first shows you concentrating on your match thirty seconds before the Midlands final and the second reveals your unpredictable scrambling, sometimes aerial, maneuvers in the Big 10 title match.

The year produced memories overflowing — watching you honored at the halftime of an Ohio State football game — traveling west to the Las Vagas Invitational — overcoming your knee injury to defeat Aaron Simpson — your focus in preparation to win the Midlands crown — missing an ice storm that devastated the East Coast to be at the Virginia Duals — the introductions at the All-Star Meet in Buffalo — the last home meet at Ohio State — a state and Big 10 Title within twenty four hours — the last seconds of your NCAA quarterfinal match — the spectacular final with family and friends present — a dad's dream!

This album depicts what I saw — a record to share with your children — I was proud to be "in your corner!"

Dad
July 1998

1998 NCAA Wrestling Champions

Front row, from left: 118 – Teague Moore, Oklahoma State;
126 – Eric Guerrero, Oklahoma State; 134 – Mark Ironside, Iowa;
142 – Jeff McGinness, Iowa; 150 – Eric Siebert, Illinois;
Back row, from left: 158 – Dwight Gardner, OhioUniversity;
167 – Joe Williams, Iowa; 177 – Mitch Clark, Ohio State;
190 – Tim Hartung, Minnesota; 275 – Stephen Neal, Cal Bakersfield

About the Authors

Mitch Clark is a native of Canton, New York. As a wrestler for Ohio State University, where he studied sports marketing, he was the 1998 NCAA Division I national champion and a two-time Big Ten champion at 177 pounds. He is an assistant coach for the Buckeyes and lives in Columbus, Ohio.

Scott Conroe is a native of Potsdam, New York. He received a bachelor's degree in English from St. Lawrence University and a master's degree in communication from Cornell University. A newspaper writer and editor for many years, he works as a free-lance writer and is a member of the New York State Intercollegiate Wrestling Coaches Hall of Fame. He lives in Cortland, New York.

Scott Conroe and Mitch Clark, January 1999